Contents

Dedication & Acknowledgements

To my wonderful, patient and resilient husband, Gareth, for helping me to realise that the knowledge I have gained could really help others on their journey. Thank you for putting up with my strange quirks, impetuous decisions and remaining *my* superhero.

To my parents, Jane and Carel. Although you have "slight" differences of opinion, you both had immeasurable impact on my life and you've been there for me in the most trying times. You are the most wonderful parents anyone could ask for!

To my friend and colleague, my fellow "career-warrior", a truly inspirational lady, Thando. Thank you for your humility and grace, curious and driven nature. There is a light that shines from within you which always brightens up my day

To my admirable, driven and successful cousin Shelley. Thank you for your sage advice and emotional support at a particularly challenging time in my life; learning how to be a mom, whilst still being a wife and a career woman.

And finally, to the lady whom convinced me to stick with recruitment when I was first finding my feet, Terri-Ann. We've been through our ups and downs but I will be forever grateful for the impact you had on my life and the people-savviness you taught me right from the start.

Note from the Author

Dear Reader,

The work world is a scary place. Unfortunately, there is no "how-to" guide to navigating your career journey. Each step you take is unique to you on your own route to success. But you're not alone.

In the current global economy, where qualified professionals and various skills shortages are in high demand, #HireMe! is aimed at providing the competitive advantage to young graduates and professionals, job seekers, who want to make their mark. A first ever career development survival "how-to" guide to taking control of the job search process. The advice given in this book and the stages to complete, can be revisited at every step in your career for years to come.

#HireMe includes comprehensive, yet specific and actionable *Survival Tips* required by go-getter and ambitious professionals, to establish their professional career profile, tackle their career journey and prepare them for job hunt success. Meanwhile, the steps discussed in #HireMe are also applicable to a more reserved and equally successful audience of professionals. These are individuals who don't necessarily want to climb the corporate ladder, yet, may want to experience great breadth or depth of experience and knowledge development throughout their careers.

I look forward to undertaking this adventure with you.

Nikki

"If we all did the things we are capable of, we would astound ourselves."

Thomas Edison

Introduction: Setting your Career up for Success

Times are tough and there are many challenges to achieving career success.

Never was it so difficult to find a job as it is now. Once upon a time, finishing high school with average grades, completing a degree at a local university or college, completing some sort of internship or graduate development programme and securing a stable job that would pay the bills, was an expected reality. Those days are long gone.

Overpopulation, market saturation, inadequate infrastructure, poor planning and the development of suitable, job-worthy degrees at a tertiary level, are just some of the challenges facing society. To further compound these issues, many companies strive to hire only the cream of the crop coming out of different and often very specific universities. Those individuals unable to study at the best university, who did not receive adequate support during their tertiary studies, or who only achieved average academic results, are left behind.

Some individuals face serious hardship and are unable to obtain a quality secondary or tertiary education. Various factors may impede the access to education and development of entire communities; financial, family responsibility, health, location and more. Vast unemployment and poverty are just two critical circumstances which can severely debilitate communities, where the immediate need for daily survival is far more crucial than obtaining a university degree certificate.

Some underprivileged communities are incredibly fortunate to receive sponsorship by external organisations which fund education. Some, more privileged, underprivileged communities, are even able to generate sponsorship from within the community. In either scenario, such initiatives tend to be aimed at supporting only the select individuals in the community who show promise.

Thereafter, of the individuals lucky enough to achieve a tertiary education, a small percentage may secure better paying jobs than they would back home. Unfortunately, the current status quo enables only a handful of previously disadvantaged individuals to lead a better life. This is particularly the case in South Africa.

Coming back to the communities, there is hope that the lucky individuals who prospered, will reinvest and give back. A contact of mine on LinkedIn, a gentleman named Edwin Moremi (COO at Dynamic Recovery Services), recently reinvested in his community by providing laptops to the youth. He too came from a disadvantaged background and has made it! This act of kindness was performed by Edwin with the hope of enabling and empowering the youth in their careers, via access to technology at a high school and tertiary level.

But, Edwin is just one drop in the ocean. Unfortunately, this fairy tale of hardship and beating the odds does not always have a happy ending. Despite the efforts of many youths to obtain a tertiary education, despairingly, many still find it nearly impossible to land a job and are forced to seek other alternatives to survive.

Education and finding a job are just two of the essential elements in setting your career up for success. Some of the most seasoned industry professionals struggle to tackle the job hunt and overcome barriers to change. The job market is really tough and to make a success you need to use every tool in your arsenal.

Differentiating yourself from the rest

To provide some context, this book is based on my knowledge and experience as a recruiter. In recruitment, I firmly believe in the motto: The candidate is King. As a recruiter, all you need is one great candidate. If the recruiter can proactively create multiple opportunities for that great candidate, three, four or five interviews at different clients for similar roles, the likelihood of placing that candidate is high. In addition, the candidate is afforded the opportunity to evaluate a variety of options, making them more likely to refer that recruiter to their friends and colleagues once successfully placed.

Particularly in the young graduate and/or professionals' market, I personally believe the proactive approach of recruitment by recruiters is a much smarter method of recruiting, versus a reactive approach. A reactive recruitment approach is when multiple recruitment agencies compete against once another by sourcing copious candidates, whilst all trying to fill the same role. When working with a recruiter that focuses on quantity versus quality (i.e. you are just a number), this is not to your advantage. If you are not the successful candidate for the job, you may find yourself quickly set aside and forgotten about.

So, what does this have to do with you, the job seeker? The candidate is King motto goes hand in hand with the concept of the Triple "A" candidate. A Triple A candidate, is a candidate that a recruiter will place, no matter what, because that candidate's profile is awesome, and/or, because that candidate has the exact skill set needed, a solid foundation of experience and a decent qualification.

To be a Triple A candidate, you don't need to be the *hottest thing since sliced bread*, nor, the individual who obtained all the distinctions at University. Sure, it helps, but far more important includes being an all-rounder, having street savvy or previous part-time work experience whilst studying (tutoring, promotions, waitering, bartending, selling insurance premiums on a commission-only basis, etc.), or someone who can swim even when thrown into the deep end.

Ultimately, if you want to differentiate yourself from the rest, it's very much about presentation and communication. For example, there is a young lady I am representing at the time of writing this book. She has an OK degree and OK academic results, although some not so great Matric results. What makes her a top-notch candidate, however, is how she communicates her work experience to date, both in person (humble, friendly, patient and inquisitive) and via her resume. She explains concepts in simple and easy to understand detail, and ensures her audience understands what she is trying to communicate. That's it!

What this boils down to is, to be a Triple A candidate, all you need is a decent profile and a good **attitude. <u>Survival Tip #1: It's all about attitude</u>**, includes all you need to know about how you come across when undertaking your job search.

You don't need to be No.1 to be a Triple A candidate. The topic of your professional profile will be discussed in more detail in <u>**Survival Tip #2: Putting together a ROCK STAR CV to shoot the lights out!**</u>

However, when putting together your professional profile, for example, include some solid foundation experience and some extracurricular activities, such as professional associations, the chess team, music classes, toastmasters or the debating team, going to gym, or even community involvement initiatives. Refer to actual experience via initiatives or projects, and the information should be communicated and articulated clearly and simply. You do not have to use big or fancy words to get your message across.

Preparing for success

Obtaining success in your job hunt is determined by

> (1) how clearly the job seeker positions themselves and their personal brand (which includes experience, relevant or irrelevant);

> (2) how they communicate the actual, tangible value they bring to the equation and no, not just "I'm a fast learner" (projects, initiatives and actual things you've done which tell your story);

> (3) how that message is communicated and perceived by the relevant parties;

> (4) whether the job seeker and the prospective employer are prepared to commit to one another;

> (5) and what details (salary, benefits, work preferences, etc.) the commitment requires to make it a reality.

The *expected* profile of a typical job seeker has changed a lot in recent years. I say expected, because there is a lot of pressure on job seekers, particularly graduate professionals, to tick several boxes if they are to be perceived as potential employees. Demonstrating your professional profile and experience is no longer just about submitting your curriculum vitae (CV) or resume via a job application.

To be considered as a potential candidate, you must be able to promote *(sell)* both your individual and team achievements; i.e. to describe and illuminate your ability to complete and excel at tasks on your own, whilst also being a team player. Every individual needs some form of digital, personal brand, and professional profile, which talks to their individual skill set and achievements. In addition, adopting proactive strategies to approaching the job market and getting ahead of the pack.

Again, not everyone is the same. Some individuals will have far more detailed and "loud" professional and digital profiles. Others, will have less detailed, far more concise and far less verbose professional and digital profiles. What is one person's personal brand (loud, ambitious and va-va-voom about their achievements), may differ dramatically from another individual, who is just as successful in their career to date, but more conservative in how they communicate their personal brand to the world.

With the more conservative approach, having only a professional and digital profile with a few one-liners, plus a CV, is perfect! What I am emphasising is: if you have a professional, digital profile, you are enabling recruiters and hiring managers to ***find you.*** This is a far more proactive approach to tackling your career, versus *you* having to apply to every job known to man, without success.

You never know when that perfect job might come along and often it is when you least expect it. To be further discussed in **Survival Tip 3: If you're not online, you don't exist.**

Meanwhile, sometimes you don't need to be the one doing the selling and you can align yourself to a strategic partner who will do so on your behalf. Aka – the recruiter! As a young graduate or professional, you will find that often, recruiters, particularly agency recruiters, are excellent doorways into corporates. If you are undertaking your job hunt on your own, strategic partners may include colleagues and key contacts in your professional network. I recommend a combination of both. This will be discussed in **Survival Tip #4: Starting your job hunt – Getting ahead of the pack through strategic partnership** and in **Survival Tip #5: All about who you know – use those Networks!**

Throughout the job search, I emphasise how important your *ability to communicate* is. Building and showcasing who you are and what you can bring to the table is very much a combination of both verbal and non-verbal communication. From communicating your interest in the role to the company or the recruiter, communicating your achievements and experience, to communicating, establishing and clarifying your expectations up front. Clarifying expectations from the beginning of your job hunt will greatly reduce the chance for any issues, misunderstandings or time wastage when job hunting.

When preparing for the interview, your ability to communicate and present yourself is critical. Unfortunately, the interview is the one experience which can be quite unpleasant for most, especially if you don't like public speaking or selling yourself.

But, dominating the interview is a necessary evil and a technique you must learn, soon.

You don't have to be loud and ambitious, to come across as assertive. In fact, often the less boisterous (i.e. noisy) individuals who calmly answer interview questions in a logical manner and provide just the right amount of detail around their experience or achievements, are those who get the job. To be discussed in **Survival Tip #7: It's time… DOMINATING the interview!**

Setting your career up for success starts years before you first enter the job market, but it doesn't mean you can't add a few things to your resume once you're in the corporate world. Organisations aren't just looking for the super bright, overachievers anymore. Companies want to hire balanced individuals who demonstrate a diversity of role-specific technical skills alongside softer skills. Individuals who can, for example, influence others in the workplace, achieve both individually and as part of a team, who take pride in their work and go the extra mile to deliver quality, and who have the right combination of technical know-how and emotional intelligence (EQ).

The requirements of various roles are also different. Some more technical or specialist roles may require more, or less, stakeholder engagement and technical ability. Some administrative or operational roles require a far more routine and less dynamic approach. Even different sales roles require varying levels of "loudness" to secure the deal. Every organisation and business unit has its nuances. Whether you are the go-getter achiever, or the worker bee, every professional contributes to the bigger picture and the bottom line in their own unique way.

When taking your career to the next level, there are several add-ons to your professional profile, which can give you the advantage and which hiring managers specifically look for in a prospective job seeker. In my final chapter and as part of the career development value-add for #HireMe!, at the end of the book I've included a chapter called: <u>**The inside scoop: What do hiring managers look for in the "best candidate for the job"?**</u>

I had a lot of fun putting this chapter together. It allowed me to the opportunity to interview and chat to several, vastly different hiring managers from different industries about what gets them excited regarding the best candidate for the job. The results from my research were diverse and interesting, yet resonate what I've already mentioned about the Triple A candidate: being Triple A is not about being No.1 or being the best. Being Triple A simply means good communication, good presentation and a good attitude. From the innovator to the administrator, anyone has the potential to be Triple A.

To all the parents: expose your child to new and diverse experiences as young as possible, whilst accepting their individualities. I don't mean try turning your children into the next Tiger Woods or Serena Williams. Rather, do everything you can to give your child a well-balanced and well-rounded upbringing. If they are social animals from day one, great! If not, let them try their hand at other things and find something they are passionate about. Allow your child the opportunity to explore and be diverse, or, explore and specialise. Make them do chores and teach them the value of money. This teaches accountability and goes a long way to how they behave as adults.

To the graduate professional job seeker: to make it in the work world, you must develop a thick skin. You might come from a home, praised by friends and family for every little achievement. Going into the work environment, to a manager who just wants you to deliver, can be quite a shock to the system. That manager isn't going to congratulate you for your every task completed. Why? Because that is your job. That is why they hired you in the first place. You will need to learn to self-praise along the way.

First-time job seekers: Be realistic and drop the attitude

If this is the first time you are trying to get into the job market, you're probably still trying to figure things out. You don't know where your career is headed, but because you have a degree, you might think you deserve a job and a fat pay cheque. It isn't going to happen! Even if the first job isn't your dream job, always remember: it's a foot in the door. Any form of work experience is better than no experience.

Insurance companies, for example, are always looking for sales people happy to work on a commission-only basis. If you're studying towards a software, engineering or mathematical degree which requires coding of some sort, there are so many online websites, local and international, where you can sell your coding abilities, even website development, for a few bucks. These days, you can even create an advert on a Facebook community group to sell your expertise or abilities! This makes for great practical experience for you! Even if it is just part-time, any form of work experience teaches you valuable skills and adds value to your CV.

Once you have three to six months' work experience, it already makes finding another job, a lot easier! Again, if you are currently studying towards completing your degree, get part-time work experience now! It shows that you are proactive and a hard worker. It also provides you with valuable skills that none of your peers might have. Even if you must volunteer and not get paid, do it! To make your job search easier and to be the preferred candidate in relation to your peers, any form of work experience can make the difference.

For experienced individuals looking to *completely change* their specialisation or career path, you will need to approach the job search in stages. More than likely, you won't be able to change course overnight and you will need to consider a sacrifice in salary. Essentially, you will be starting from the bottom again and cannot expect massive hand-outs.

If you're able to get yourself into the right environment, division or company, the pursuit of your dream job is one step closer. Once you've grown your knowledge and experience in line with, or, similar to where you believe your career is headed, options will begin opening up to you. Then you take the next step. Be patient and realistic with yourself.

Through #HireMe!, I look forward to providing you with the tools and techniques to not only find a job, but to enable you to pick and choose which job will become your career path. Like anything in life, it takes work, perseverance and getting out of your comfort zone. Just remember, this book provides guidelines. It is up you, to make it a reality. Let's get started!

"If you want the cooperation of humans around you, you must make them feel they are important – and you do that by being genuine and humble."

Nelson Mandela

SURVIVAL TIP #1: It's all about attitude

Ever heard of the saying: *First impressions last forever?*

In this first chapter, I'd like to touch on a sensitive subject; attitude. Attitude in relation to this book, is the way in which you come across in your job search. The right attitude can be the winning formula to successfully landing your job, especially if it is your first job. If you're the extroverted super-star, you might think quite a lot of yourself and your abilities, Whether consciously or subconsciously you might believe that you are such a rock star, because you received all "A"s during your studies. Thus, of course, you will land you that dream job.

Wrong. I can promise you, you probably won't. In fact, it is in such situations where the slightly more subdued, yet assertive and humble individuals tend to thrive. Any sort of attitude in a job seeker, no matter their career level or age, is going to immediately put-off prospective employers and recruiters. Worst part, you may not even realise you have an attitude!

In 2015, a study was conducted in the United Kingdom across several employers and different industries to identify critical success factors to landing a job. 90% of the participants in the study stated that the No.1 make or break criteria employers look for in a prospective employee is the right attitude.

Attitude is a combination of both verbal and non-verbal communication. For example, it can be the overconfident way you discuss certain topics, how you tend to talk *over* or interrupt your interviewers, how you raise yourself up on a pedestal or criticise your fellow employees, or by simply dismissing the opinions of others.

Alternatively, and on the non-verbal side, it could include slouching in your chair, not maintaining eye contact, twiddling your thumbs, fidgeting, rocking back and forth in your chair, giving a half-hearted handshake when greeting your interviewers, chewing bubble gum, or looking like you just rolled out of bed to attend an interview.

As a job seeker, your attitude during the job search can have both positive and negative repercussions. In my experience, when dealing with an individual who comes across as rude, overly confident in their abilities, ludicrous in their salary expectations with limited work experience, or who just doesn't seem committed to the job search process yet wants to gain options to get a big salary increase, I refer to that as acting "entitled".

No matter who you are, when dealing with an individual who comes across as nasty, rude, arrogant, lack-lustre, entitled or impatient, it doesn't bode well for future interaction and communication. I apologise for harping on about this point, but it really can make or break your job search. Many job seekers may not even realise that they have an attitude!

At the time of writing this book I was assisting another young lady, an individual from my #HireAGrad initiative. #HireAGrad is a campaign I launched during the pre-launch marketing of #HireMe! #HireAGrad is focused on upskilling young graduate professionals via immediate, industry required scarce skills, making these individuals more employable. Thereafter, assisting them with securing employment. This young lady didn't realise it, but there were certain ways in which she behaved and said things, which immediately alerted me to the fact that she had a bit of an attitude. She just thought she was being assertive, but to prospective employers, she was perceived as arrogant.

To prepare her for the job search success, I held a blunt and uncomfortable conversation with her around attitude, as this was impacting her ability to succeed. I still remember asking her what challenges she had answering questions in interviews and her response was, "Oh nothing. Nothing I can think of, no." To which I responded: "So why don't you have a job yet?"

This girl was a potential Triple A candidate, but her attitude was letting her down.

My advice, whether young, bright and bushy-tailed, or an experienced individual, you need to be very aware of how you come across to others. As a young professional, be very careful of thinking:

"Wow, I am a rock star! I've got my university degree and I'm ready to take on the work world. Now give me a job and pay me for my years of [theoretical] knowledge!"

Or, in the case of more Senior individuals:

"This company can't survive without me and my skills. They are lucky to have me and they must pay!"

A huge mistake that both new and experienced job seekers make, is to assume that they are the only person for the job and that the company won't be able to find anyone better. Wrong. That's why South Africa has such a high unemployment rate;

surplus skilled graduate professionals to the number of jobs currently available. There are plenty of qualified individuals in the job market who would fight tooth and nail for an opportunity in their respective fields.

Don't misunderstand though. Companies definitely want individuals with enthusiasm and drive! But, being the best and the brightest is not just about scholastic or extramural achievements. It is far more than that.

#HireMe! is meant to serve as a guide to help individuals understand and navigate their path through the job search journey. The first step in that journey is self-evaluation and constructive self-criticism.

You need to ask yourself: Are you someone that a company would actually want to hire?

When selecting graduates from a massive pool of applicants, organisations look for individual qualities which will enable each graduate to integrate into the work environment, work well with others, handle conflict in a positive manner and get the job done no matter what. Thus, far more attractive traits in a prospective employee include humility, a thirst for knowledge and skills, a can-do attitude and an openness to constructive criticism.

Although companies want to see the individual value that each job applicant could potentially bring to the table, they also want to see that you are someone they can work with. When a company hires an individual with a bad attitude, whether lazy, disinterested or arrogant, they are bringing someone into their company or team who has the potential to poison the existing dynamic. No company wants that, no matter how *out-of-this-world* the prospective employee might be.

My personal belief, and from what I have seen, is that once you start behaving with humility, friendliness, dignity and an eagerness to learn, then you already have a foot in the door. So simple, yet can make or break your job application.

This is also true when beginning your interactions with recruiters – the gatekeepers to opportunities. Recruiters are ridiculously busy people and often completely overworked. In South Africa, corporate recruitment teams tend to be totally understaffed. Most organisations view recruitment divisions as "cost centres" because these divisions don't generate a profit. Most recruitment teams are allocated small budgets and cannot afford to hire enough manpower to adequately manage or respond to the number of job applications received from prospective, external job seekers.

Recruiters deal with a wide range of individuals daily, all with different attitudes and approaches to their job searches. As much as recruitment is about dealing with people, it is also an incredibly admin intensive job; reviewing CVs, sending CVs to hiring managers, setting up interviews, performing interview feedback sessions with candidates and hiring managers, arranging and conducting background checks on prospective individuals, preparing detailed offer letters, completing on-boarding procedures for new starts, and more.

When dealing with a recruiter, whether agency or corporate, the last thing you want is to treat the individual with disrespect, impatience or any other negative form of communication. These unsung heroes have more than enough to deal with daily, without further drama. All they do is click *"Delete"* on your application and your opportunity it gone.

Not only that, but they will remember you. Should your profile come across their desk again in future, or go to one of their colleagues, they will likely tell their colleague not to work with you! For example, there are candidates I remember from when I first started working in recruitment in 2010, many of which I still won't work with until this day. I remember how they behaved at the time.

Your past negative behaviour can and will have consequences for your future job search interactions.

Same goes for hiring managers. Let's say you make it past the recruitment gatekeepers and the next step is meeting the hiring manager. It appears that the manager is impressed by your skill set. You are excited! This is as good a time as ever to negotiate and sell yourself like there is no tomorrow! Let the hiring manager know why you are the best person for the job and why the company shouldn't waste time meeting with any other applicants. Right?

Yes and no. You need to be careful. There is a very fine line between coming across as confident and charming, versus sounding obnoxious. A couple of basic pointers:

1. Never criticise or compare yourself to others, whether positive or negative, as it indicates insecurity;
2. Never take all the credit for yourself for a successful initiative (unless you really were the only individual whatsoever working on the initiative), but do highlight what your key contributions to projects or initiatives were;

3. Make sure you credit other members of the team on an initiative as it shows humility; and

4. Always ensure you answer the question asked, versus going off on an irrelevant, self-inflating tangent where the hiring manager is unable to get a word in edge-wise.

In summary, when dealing with people during your job search journey bear in mind the following advice:

1. Remember that your attitude reflects both negatively and positively in your favour, so be the best person you can as you go through each step on your job search journey.

2. Behaving in a demanding or aloof manner won't help you achieve success on your job search journey, no matter your level, age, qualification or years of experience. The younger and more inexperienced you are, the more likely you are to come across as entitled. It's a big turn-off for companies. Young or experienced, you probably still have a lot to learn about each unique organisation before you're able to offer the company any real value.

3. Take each interaction on your job search journey as an opportunity to showcase the awesome person you could be, as part of an organisation's dynamic; behave with humility and dignity, treat others with the utmost respect and emphasise your eagerness to learn.

4. People don't easily forget an unpleasant experience. Burning bridges at the very beginning of your job search journey can have lasting consequences. This is especially true if you upset individuals in positions of power. Individuals in positions of power aren't just the hiring managers, but also include recruitment

gatekeepers, who may either support or prevent your application.

5. Get your attitude in check by self-evaluating. Ask yourself: would I want to hire me if I was a company? The price of being friendly and humble versus lack-lustre, impatient or demanding, can mean the difference between a *few weeks*, to a **few months** or even **years** of extensive, desperate job searching.

"Tell the world what you intend to do, but first show it."

Napoleon Hill

SURVIVAL TIP #2: Putting together a ROCK STAR CV to shoot the lights out!

When starting the job hunt you only have one chance to make a first impression. More than likely this will be through a professional, detailed and concise curriculum vitae (CV). What is the point of spending years of effort investing in your studies, work experience and gaining professional achievements, if you are not going to use that information to build your own personal sales' pitch? You are the one in the driver's seat and can determine how best to campaign your professional profile!

Just think of Apple, Coca-Cola or Mercedes Benz. Or bringing it a little closer to home; Nandos, Omo, Jik, Dove, Castle Lager, Web Africa or even FNB? What makes everyone want to buy their products? Quality is one factor. More so, it is about the uniqueness of how these companies market their products and the *perceived quality* by the consumer, because of the marketing campaign.

Like any Company selling and promoting its products, if you want to gain traction in the local job market and obtain the most value from your efforts, you need to invest the time in developing your personal profile and professional brand. You do not need to be the loudest or most flamboyant, but you do need some form of presence.

If you cut corners when building your professional profile, it sends a very clear message to any potential future employers: You are not serious, couldn't care less about the job hunt, or that the quality of what you deliver is not good. For example, you don't bother performing a basic spell check on your CV…

Time to get serious. It is hard enough to find a job in the current economy, never mind a job you actually like! It's time to apply some basic marketing principles to how you develop your professional profile. If you want to get the edge over your competition, you need to dig deep and think.

One myth I would like to expel: You aren't going to get a job simply because you obtained a degree or diploma. Jobs are scarce and in high demand. It takes a lot more than a pretty piece of paper to create a resounding first impression. Evaluating your professional profile as though it were your own personal marketing campaign, let's look at how you can promote yourself and your brand to the market. For example:

1. **The devil is in the detail:** You need to identify all the specific and technical details of what you have done during your career; i.e. your skill set. This includes your education, employment history, roles and responsibilities, specific initiatives or projects worked on, computer skills, software tools or technologies you have experience of, your key proficiencies or areas of specialisation, any extracurricular activities which might speak to leadership or your ability to work well in a team and so forth.

2. **Presentation, presentation, presentation!** You need to need to decide on the layout of all these details. How will these details BEST attract the intended attention you are looking to gain? Given your profession or career choice, will using one CV format versus another make a difference to how your application is considered? Some lengthier and more creative versus something short, concise and professional? Looking at the keywords which companies use when advertising their vacancies, is your CV mentioning the same talking

points? Of course, you must have obtained the relevant experience before listing it in your CV. Is there anything else you haven't thought of which might position your CV better, like extracurricular activities which showcase your leadership or team work abilities? Perhaps a hobby or interest which enables you to perform your job better?

3. **Who, how, what, when and why?** You need to identify who your potential target audience is and finalise the complete presentation of your profile, which will go to market. To get your CV to market, you need to decide where and on which platforms you might be able to obtain the best and the most relevant exposure for your profile; i.e. the most hits. For example, a professionals networking site, professional workshops or seminars, career websites, online forums, direct applications via email, fax, or phoning the hiring manager or recruiter directly to pitch your profile to them.

4. **Learning how to sell YOU!** Finally, you need to learn how to sell yourself to prospective employers and recruiters. This is partly in how your final CV is presented, but even more so in the opportunities you identify by networking and having many, many conversations and cups of coffee. To be discussed more **in** Survival Tip #4: Starting your job hunt – Getting ahead of the pack through strategic partnership and in Survival Tip #6: All about who you know – use those Networks! For example, digital networking websites such as LinkedIn can be very valuable for professionals wanting to gain access to other professionals. LinkedIn enables you to make direct contact with other individuals from around the world, whether to ask for advice, have conversations, or to

even ask about possible available company vacancies, once the correct introductions are made.

Learning how to sell yourself is one of the most difficult lessons in life. When undertaking your job search journey, you will need to learn how to sell yourself both in paper and in person. If you don't learn how to, or cannot sell yourself, you will always settle for second or third best. Why? Because you will be too scared to push for first; to state why you are the best person for the job. *Selling yourself is not just natural skill. It is a **learnt behaviour** and it takes time and practise.*

Side Note: *I personally recommend writing a script and practising talking to yourself from time-to-time in front of the mirror. By doing so, you may quickly realise certain detrimental verbal and non-verbal cues which influence the way you communicate. For example, if you frown and rush through a statement every time you are discussing an important point, this might result in a negative impact. People won't realise the importance of the point you've just made and might wonder why you seem so nervous. Neither of these reactions are positive reinforcement.*

In addition, when practising in front of the mirror, take a deep breath, pause and smile for effect. Then go for it! The more deliberate you become in way you speak and pronounce your words, in each interaction you have with others, the better a communicator you will become.

Getting back to putting together a CV, I've included a basic template below. Other easy to use templates can be found at https://www.visualcv.com/ or http://vizualize.me/. VisualCV.com comes highly recommended by several international organisations, including Forbes, Mashable, CNN,

Wall Street Journal, and more. These tools can help quickly convert and capture the look and feel of the CV you would like to use, although you would still need to do some editing.

A template is very valuable when putting together a CV because companies don't necessarily want you to reinvent the wheel by creating a complex document. Rather, they want to see a professional profile which is clear, logical and concise, whilst relaying comprehensive information as to who you are and what you are all about. This demonstrates that an individual has a clear and logical communication ability.

The easier it is to skim through and understand your CV, the more likely a recruiter or company will be interested in meeting with you. To guide your readers, I recommend including specific headings, using bullet points, summarising your experience to the key essentials and leaving out any "fluffy stuff". Fluffy stuff includes anything that is overly emotional, cannot be verified and is a description by the writer of the CV of themselves and not by an independent party, and/or is not appropriate for a CV. For example:

"John is a strong leader with a clear mind and strong goal-setting ability."

Whilst some of the information might be true, it does not tell the person reading your CV anything about you because no example is provided. If you are unable to provide an example of where you demonstrated a "clear mind and strong goal-setting ability", leave it out. However, if you include more detail after the sentence above, it may be appropriate. For example:

"John is a strong leader with a clear mind and strong goal-setting ability. He took the lead role on 3x team projects during the University 3rd and 4th year, for his Strategic Management subject, and enabled his team to achieve a consistent aggregate of 75%."

This statement makes John's goal-setting abilities seem more real, because context is provided. In your CV it is important to provide numerous examples of actual experiences, as this brings your CV to life, for the reader.

When it comes to the content of the CV, the information which is going to grab the attention of your prospective employer, I highly recommend using the template below as a guide. You might create the most beautiful CV in the world, but if the relevant content isn't there, or it is not easily understood, you probably won't get any interviews. Alternatively, if the information is not specific enough regarding your skill set, you might be invited for interviews for the wrong type of job!

Fun Fact: Less than a quarter (25%) of the CVs I receive daily include examples of actual experience gained by the individual, and more than 80% of the CVs I receive read like job specifications. It is very easy to see when a person has simply cut and pasted their current work or job description as their role summary or responsibilities. It is an immediate turn-off! It shows that you are too lazy to invest time in thinking for yourself about your experiences, to put together your CV.

CV TEMPLATE

CURRICULUM VITAE OF JACK SMITH

Full Name: Jacobus Smith	23 Sungarden Terrace, Randburg, 2010
National ID: 7767990098766	Nationality: South African
Gender: Male	August 2013
Ethnicity: White	Married: Yes + 2 Children

Putting your national identification number (ID), Gender and Ethnicity are all OPTIONAL items. Depending on where you live in the world, serious legal action could be taken against an employer if they are found to be discriminating based on ID, Gender or Ethnicity.

Executive Summary:

Remember to always put your CV in the Third Person. This comes across to employers as far more professional. Also – I would set your paragraph spacing throughout the CV to 1.15 or 1.5. This means that the lines are a little further apart and makes the much easier to read by recruiters. If all the information is squashed together, it can make for difficult reading and the recruiter is more likely to chuck your CV in the recycle bin.

- Who you are and what you want to do: **"Jack is a passionate Chartered Accountant…"**
- What your highest level/s of education are: **"… with his B.Com Honours Accounting and his Articles completed with Deloitte during 2012."**

- What industries you have any experience of: "He has worked in Financial Services Audit and Consulting environment for the past four years. During his time at University he tutored 2nd, 3rd and Honours Year students."
- What your core technical and/or computer skills are: "He has gained experience of the following tools and technologies: MS Office, AccPac, Payroll PSS, MS Excel, Pastel and various other accounting software packages."

If there is a 2nd paragraph or part to the executive summary, then just add in any companies that you have worked for, for what duration and what key duties you were involved in. If at all possible and if you are not restricted from disclosing the information, also include any key or pertinent initiatives/projects involved in. For example:

"John completed his articles with Deloitte during 2012 and his key duties included filing new accounts, creating new data entries, identifying discrepancies on a daily basis, creating reports (daily, weekly and monthly), interacting with various stakeholders, dealing with vendors in finance, etc.

Key projects included:

1. Standard Bank of South Africa – involved in the complete audit of the 2012/2013 financial year for the Personal and Business Banking division
2. MTN – advised on and managed a team of trainee article clerks for the 2013/2014 financial year audit for the client within the Customer Value Management division
3. IBM South Africa – instrumental in developing and developing a new audit methodology and

approach in line with prevailing market regulations for the 2014/2015 financial year end audit
4. Deloitte (internal project) – driver behind the Deloitte "Audit Information Security" programme, aimed at circumventing cyber security threats in relation to audit initiatives offered to all key clientele

Education:

*See below for each individual entry and remember to INCLUDE any and all distinctions, achievements, thesis information, etc. Always **bold achievements** and **distinctions** so that they immediately stand out to the client. Every bit of information you include in your CV makes your profile more marketable to potential employers and provides talking points for the interviewers when you attend the interview.*

***PS**: If you want to control the interview, ensure the information in your CV is recent and relevant and that you have gone through any listed examples a number of times. If you direct the employers around what topics to ask questions about, then you are sitting in the driver's seat.*

- Institution
- Period
- Qualification
- Thesis Topic (for Honours, Masters or PhD)
- **Distinctions**

EXAMPLE:

- Institution   University of Cape Town
- Period   2008 - 2011

- Qualification   B.Com Honours (Accounting) with Financial Mathematics *(with distinction)*
- Thesis Topic   (optional)   Completed articles through Deloitte (2012 to 2014)
- **Distinctions   5x Distinctions – Accounting 101 & 201, Management Theory 101, Financial Mathematics 101 & 201**

Additional Certifications:

See below for each individual entry and remember to INCLUDE any and all distinctions, achievements, etc.:

- Institution
- Year Achieved
- Qualification
- Distinctions or Achievements

EXAMPLE

- Institution   International Financial Managers Institute (IFMI)
- Year Achieved   2010
- Qualification   Core Concepts of Accounting
- **Achievements Top Speaker as part of the Financial Manager Debate Programme for the Core Concepts of Accounting Certification**

Professional Memberships:

Do this for each entry:

- Institution
- Period
- Membership

EXAMPLE

- Institution   South   African   Institute   of
  Chartered Accountants (SAICA)
- Period   2014 to Current
- Membership   Chartered   Accountant –
  Membership No. 22222222

Core Skills & Abilities (Key Strengths):

This is a tricky one and you might need to get family to help as we are often not that good at identifying our own key strengths. Look at the first paragraph of your executive summary if you have completed it. Again, this should not include anything fluffy or emotional, but rather should be focused on actual competencies, skills or knowledge you may have. For example:

- Chartered Accountant
- AccPacc
- Accounting Software Packages
- Pastel
- MS Office
- MS Excel (advanced)
- Financial Services Audit / Commerce and Consulting
- Financial Mathematics

Handy Tip: remember to move your headings to the next page if they are hanging right at the bottom of a page without any content thereafter. It looks far more professional when the heading starts on a new page, instead of at the bottom of the previous page and doesn't leave your readers hanging. Press the CTRL and Enter buttons at the same time to insert a page break before each new heading or go to the MS Word Menu, click on "Insert" and then click on "Page Break".

Employment History:

- Employer
- Division
- Entire Period (per employer)
- Job Title / Designation
- Responsibilities
    - Creating Reports (daily, weekly and monthly)
    - Creating new data entries
    - Finalizing audit entries for various year end audits, from 2012 to 2015

Try to include a minimum of at least 5 to 10 responsibilities per job function. It can be incredibly frustrating for potential employers or recruiters going through your CV if the information is limited. This would mean they might have to contact you for additional information. Given the incredible volumes of CVs these individuals receive on a daily basis and the effort it would take to then correspond with you, they are more likely to simply click "Delete" on your application.

- Major Projects/Initiatives
    - Standard Bank of South Africa – involved in the complete audit of the 2012/2013 financial year for the Personal and Business Banking division
    - MTN – advised on and managed a team of trainee article clerks for the 2013/2014 financial year audit for the client within the Customer Value Management division
    - IBM South Africa – instrumental in developing and developing a new audit methodology and approach in line with prevailing market regulations for the 2014/2015 financial year end audit

- o Deloitte (internal project) – driver behind the Deloitte "Audit Information Security" programme, aimed at circumventing cyber security threats in relation to audit initiatives offered to all key clientele

- Reason for leaving –

Copy and paste the above for each employment entry. If each entry is within a different division, but at the same employer, then simply change employer to "Division" each time there is a new division with a new period and new duties. This is particularly relevant for individuals whom have worked in many different roles in any one company. For example:

- Division
- Period (per division)
- Job Title / Designation
- Responsibilities

References:

- Available on request

For the sake of confidentiality, it is a far better option to ONLY send reference details through to the recruiter or potential future employer once they are requested. Otherwise the information has the potential to become freely available to pretty any recruiter via whichever job portals you have uploaded your CV to.

"It always seems impossible until it's done."

Nelson Mandela

SURVIVAL TIP #3: If you're not online, you don't exist

In today's world, a world where the current job market is quickly being taken over by young and dynamic technologically inclined youths, a digital, professional profile is crucial. Per several recent surveys including a 2016 CareerBuilder survey, research found that 53% of employers will verify your existence by checking for an online profile. In addition, 60% of hiring managers utilise social media to research your professional profile to verify whether what you are putting on your CV matches what you are reflecting on your online profile. Simultaneously, a vast majority of prospective employers and recruiters now use social media as a powerful tool for interacting directly with prospective employees.

However, you could choose to avoid any potential pitfalls which come with having all your personal, professional information online and go the traditional, old school job board or newspaper route. You would be doing yourself a disservice. I always check online to see whether my candidates have a LinkedIn or Facebook profile. This is to both verify content and their existence. I always find it quite strange, and a bit suspect, when I can't find a candidate or prospective job seeker anywhere online, especially those in the "under 40" age bracket.

Pros and cons of having a social media presence

A social media profile enables you to be connected; to stay in contact with anyone anywhere in the world, regardless of physical boundaries. When job hunting, a social media profile enables you to take advantage of any connections you might have (and their connections) by eliminating barriers to interaction. Several social media platforms have established access restrictions to protect users, and which both allow and limit the number of users one can communicate with.

If you were to compare Twitter and LinkedIn, for example, Twitter allows you to be free as a bird (pardon the pun) regarding whom you can interact with or follow. For example, if you wanted to tag to Rihanna or Casper Nyovest in a "tweet", you could.

Whereas, LinkedIn only allows several levels of interaction with 1st or immediate connections and group connections, versus 2nd and 3rd level connections. 2nd and 3rd level connections are the immediate or 1st level connections of your 1st level connections, but not directly connected to you; i.e. friends of your friends, with whom you are already connected. For example, you know Ron and Ron is connected to Sipho. You don't directly know Sipho and you are not connected to Sipho on LinkedIn. Thus, you are connected *indirectly* to Sipho via Ron. Sipho is a 2nd Level Connection.

Everyone Ron is directly connected to, whom you are not directly connected to, would be a 2nd level connection to you. Then, everyone Sipho is connected to, whom you are not connected to, is a 3rd level connection to you. For example, Sipho is connected to Pravani, but neither yourself nor Ron are connected to Pravani. Pravani is a 3rd level connection to you and a 2nd level connection to Ron.

For example:

You ➔ (1st Level) Ron ➔ (2nd Level) Sipho ➔ (3rd Level) Pravani

On LinkedIn, if you want to gain access to more immediate, individual users, you need to invite more users to connect with you and vice versa. This allows you to increase your reach to other users and to any posts or content these networks might have created (blogs, articles, posts, sound bites, videos, etc.). Such content is incredibly important because it's what is front of mind for connections within your network at that moment. Furthermore, the content your connections are sharing could also provide you with some good conversation starters in an interview.

However, if you try to connect to too many users who you don't know or who decline your invitations, LinkedIn sends you a reprimanding email and may even suspend your account. If your account is suspended and/or you are limited to the number of LinkedIn connection requests you are allowed to send, you are then expected to utilise the paid prescriptions which allow you access to a specific number of "InMails" (direct emails) which you may send to LinkedIn users per month. In addition, to stop connecting with people you don't know, or LinkedIn will kick you off their site.

Personally, it defeats the point of an open and transparent social media or global professionals network, but LinkedIn has to make money off their product somehow!

Ultimately, the great thing about social media is that you can pretty much communicate with anyone you want, at any time, even if you are sitting in front of your computer in your pyjamas! Old boundaries have dissipated and you no longer have to wait weeks or months to receive a response in the physical post box.

Social media has broken down and eradicated vast control which corporates previously enjoyed when it came to the recruitment lifecycle or job search process. Previously, for you to gain access to a particular person at a specific company, you would have needed some connection; a friend or colleague, a formal job application on your part, and so forth. You probably wouldn't have known who headed up which division in a particular company, even though this information would have made the world of difference to your application.

Times have changed and the competition is getting tougher. Now it is crucially important to your job hunt that you know the "who", "what" and "where", to make a real impression. Thanks to social media platforms and the pursuit of your job hunt, you have direct access to key influencers whom you may not have known existed. Depending on the size of your social media network and the pace at which you add contacts to your existing network, the number of individuals, or key stakeholders, you could be interacting with daily is unlimited.

On the flip side of the coin, when you decide to put your personal information online you lose ownership of that information. Although there are all sorts of disclaimers that companies won't use your information without your consent, the data you provide will sit in the web forever and ever. Even if you try delete certain information which you previously saved online, there will always be a backup computer server somewhere, which retains the information as a form of fail-safe. It's nearly impossible to really delete anything these days.

What does this mean for you? If you haven't already, when you do finally decide to put your social profile online you must be certain of what information you are comfortable with sharing, knowing that there will be an imprint of that information on the web until the end of time. This includes everything from the intimate details of your personal profile, through to the types of comments or posts you might make. Your social profile will become your personal, social brand, which will in turn influence and/or become your professional, networking brand.

When building your professional, personal brand, be wary of what content you decide to post or discuss. Some online individuals are incredibly vocal on their social profiles and others share only minimum details. This content could really help to sell your personal brand/or become a major thorn in your side.

For example, future employers may evaluate the topics you are posting about and whether you are aware of what is happening in the world around you. A question you need to ask yourself is, "Does my social profile show that I am aware of the bigger picture or does it make me sound like an opinionated bigot?" *Enter stage right... Penny Sparrow...*

When developing your social brand, just as with your CV, presentation is paramount. You have the opportunity to put together a profile which makes you sound like an absolute rock star, or an ill-educated and lazy individual. If, for example, you don't bother ensuring your online profile has proper grammar and no spelling mistakes, this once more sends a negative message to the prospective hiring manager.

Important to note: *When putting together content which you post via your social media profile, you need to be aware of possible reputational risk for yourself, and whether there may be any legal ramifications. There is still a lot of case law to be* *established around the use and distribution of information online. One thing is for certain: If you suddenly start spouting outdated, discriminatory, obscene or defamatory views on any given topic or person, you could quickly find yourself in trouble.*

Your digital, professional and/or social profile should be a close replica of your resume. When a prospective employer reviews your social media profile versus your CV, you don't want any questionable discrepancies between the two. You must avoid including any information on your profile which could paint you in a negative light and you must ensure that the information posted is 100% correct. To make it easier for yourself, once your CV is complete, simply select which pieces of information you are going to take from your CV and then paste these sections onto your social profile. This way you avoid content discrepancies between your CV and your digital, professional profile. In addition, it cuts down on time wastage involved in recreating and retyping your digital, professional or social profile from scratch.

My advice:

- **Do** include a summary of your education, your academic, career and/or social achievements, your role or technology specific core skills (not the fluffy stuff) and any pertinent projects or initiatives which demonstrate your abilities, and which you are allowed to share without any confidentiality repercussions from any previous employers.
- **Don't** include your contact details, any form of national identification or passport number, the names and contact details of your references, your student number/s or any other form of identification. Why? The last thing you want to do is put so much information about yourself online, accessible to anyone, which

might easily result in someone duplicating your profile, gaining access to any of your accounts and potentially committing fraud.

On the point of references and referrals: Social media platforms like LinkedIn have a couple of ways in which you can either give or receive a reference. References help you establish credibility and verify your existence; i.e. there are other people online who know you, who may have worked with you and can comment on your abilities. On LinkedIn, referees can either (1) write an original, detailed reference which is first sent to you and you have the option to accept the reference to be posted to your social media profile or not, or (2) individuals can choose to endorse you for what LinkedIn or you have listed as your core skills.

To endorse your skills, a LinkedIn connection goes onto your LinkedIn profile page, scrolls down to the section of your profile named "Skills and Endorsements", and clicks on one of the buttons next to the various key words (core skills) which you've listed, which he or she wants to endorse you for. For example, if I want to endorse my friend Thandi for "Customer Service", I would navigate to her LinkedIn profile page and either click on the existing "Customer Service" button under the heading "Skills & Endorsements" or I have the option to add an entirely new core skill to her profile. The more endorsements Thandi receives, the more favourable her profile looks to a potential future employer.

In summary, once your digital, professional or social media profile is setup and your CV is done and dusted, it's time for the next step in your job search. How are you going to get your CV out there? How are you going to apply for or attract prospective employers? Your social media profile confirms your existence and, if done correctly, will boost and verify your professional profile to potential future employers. In addition, if you continuously keep your social media or digital, professional profile up to date, you may find that employers or recruiters reach out to you with opportunities, even when you're not looking! This is a great position to be in. You never know when the next step in your career might be right around the corner.

"My humanity is bound up in yours, for we can only be human together."

Archbishop Desmond Tutu

SURVIVAL TIP #4: Starting your job hunt – Getting ahead of the pack through strategic partnership

You've put together an amazing CV and a rock star digital, professional profile - you are ready to get moving! Next obstacle: where do you start looking for jobs? At this point, many job seekers would logon to an online job board (In South Africa we have: Careers24, PNET, CareerJunction, Indeed, etc.), create a user profile, potentially apply for between one to five jobs, then sit back and wait for someone to get back to them.

It resembles a fisherman, throwing his fishing line out to sea and waiting (and waiting) for something to happen. Or a gambler, who continues to throw his money into slot machines, waiting for his one chance to get lucky and win. This is a very reactive approach to your job search, waiting for someone else to determine your fate for you. It can be incredibly demoralising. Therefore, you need to take a more proactive approach to your job search.

Beware of spray and pray

If you are going to make use of traditional job boards, beware of spray and pray. Some job seekers are aggressive or desperate on job boards applying to many, many jobs, both relevant and irrelevant. This tells a recruiter, whether in a company or in an agency, that you don't know what you want, that you are desperate and that you are a high-risk candidate who will jump at the next best opportunity, leaving your current company high and dry.

Job seekers who spray and pray are not the candidates that professional recruiters or corporates want to work with and can cause a lot of trouble for agency recruiters. What tends to happen, is that many agencies receive the same candidate's CV. If this is a potential Triple A candidate, many of these agencies will interview the candidate and prepare an application to be sent to various, relevant corporate clients.

Each agency recruiter then painstakingly prepares the job seeker professional profile or CV in their company's format, each recruiter highlighting the core skills they've identified in the candidate. Next, all these agency recruiters submit the same job seeker's CV, but in different formats and with different core skills, to the same vacancy at a company.

The company's recruitment team or hiring manager starts sifting through all the CVs they've received. They notice that the same candidate's profile has come into their inbox from several, different agency recruiters. Each CV is in a different format, highlighting different aspects of the same candidate's profile. Some of the CVs even contain completely different information, compared to the others.

To you the job seeker, this might seem fine at first. The more agencies you work with, the higher the likelihood of securing a job, even if they submit you for the same profile? Not necessarily. When a candidate works with multiple agencies and doesn't inform other agencies of whom he or she is working with, or where their CV has already been sent, it is a complete waste of everyone's time. As a hiring manager or corporate recruiter, these individuals have far more important things to do than to figure out which is the most correct CV, or which duplicate CV best suits the role.

To the company, it sends a clear message that this candidate is desperate and has no loyalty to any of the recruiters representing him or her. Meanwhile, it casts a shadow of doubt on the abilities of the agency recruiters. Why did these agency recruiters not do their homework properly? Did they not ask the job seeker whether their CV was already submitted to that role, or to that company?

Even though the job seeker is often the one that does not disclose the required information, the agency recruiter tends to sit with the blame. Job seekers don't realise this, but such negative interactions between the agency recruiter and the company often have long-lasting, negative ripple effects on the relationship. As a candidate endorsed by any agency recruiter, you represent the reputation of that agency to the companies (potential, prospective employers) to which you are introduced

Long story short: the buck stops with the candidate. It is up to you to be vigilant with your personal information and to be completely truthful, honest and transparent. This bodes well for a long-term relationship with your agency recruiter and/or the company at which you are interviewing.

On another note, if an agency recruiter suddenly contacts you out of the blue for an interview with a company, of which you were unaware, then **you** need to hold that agency recruiter accountable. There are some agency recruiters who genuinely want to assist you and take pride in their work. However, there are also those who themselves apply the spray and pray method, even when they haven't spoken to the candidate before! You need to avoid these at all costs.

If not spray and pray, then what?

Getting back on track, how can you get ahead of the pack? As mentioned in the introduction of this book and Survival Tip #1, there are far more candidates entering the job market, than there are jobs available. In some niche or scarce markets there is still high demand, but definitely not enough relevant or qualified skill sets. Unfortunately, many companies only want candidates who have relevant work experience. Again, this makes it incredibly tough to get going on your job hunt and you will need to take some form of initiative.

It is at this point that I recommend putting together a project plan of sorts. A project plan includes specific steps, measurable objectives and timelines. For example:

1. Identify what it is you want to achieve and over what period – i.e. goal or target setting over the short term, medium term and long term.
2. Identify your networks and ways in which to reach these networks (this will be discussed in the next chapter in depth) – i.e. identifying your broad, potential target segment.
3. Identify and match your skill set and values to specific companies in your relevant job market. These could also include any specific companies that you may really want to work for. Passion for and knowledge of a company will always come in handy – i.e. selecting your target market.
4. Identify if and who has the potential to be your strategic partner in your quest. Remember that you are not an

island. As with any project or initiative there may be subject matter experts (SMEs) who could assist you in obtaining the best results by leveraging off years of industry experience in the field you want to get into. In this scenario, SMEs may include industry- or role-specific recruiters, industry colleagues or hiring managers. These are individuals who can open doors specific to your skill set and ambitions – i.e. identifying and partnering with your SMEs.

5. Finally, don't procrastinate, try to overcome any shyness or inhibitions (this is where you need to learn to sell yourself...) and move it! Once some basic homework is done and you've identified a few individuals who might be able to either partner with you on this journey or point you in the right direction for opportunities, take the leap, reach out and go!

Below I have included an exercise which I highly recommend you, the job seeker, undertake as a starting point to your job search journey. Should you work with an agency recruiter, they will likely ask you a combination of the below questions to better understand your professional profile and to prompt your thinking around the next steps in your career journey.

Identify and match your skill set to companies in the job market.

Now that you've created your CV, review your profile and identify the following:

1. What are your core job and industry specific skills (not fluffy stuff)?
2. As part of your current job, past job or past studies, what did you really enjoy doing?
3. What didn't you enjoy doing?

4. Are you particularly technical in any specific way that stands out? For example, creating a presentation, building a complex excel spreadsheet, or an amazing ability to organise and structure things?
5. What type of role have you played in the past on projects (leader, team player, strategy-man, etc.)?
6. Does your skill set apply to any specific industries or environments? Try to be as specific as you can as this provides a good starting point. The more generalised you are, the vaguer and more generalised your job hunt. You want to be specific and targeted. For example:
   a. Engineering and what type of engineering?
   b. Financial and what type of financial?
   c. Scientific and what type of scientific?
   d. Research and what type of research?
   e. Business Management and what type of business?
   f. Other?
7. Why do you think your skill set fits into this bracket? Think of specific examples. If you can't think of any examples, you need to start the process again, as you might be on the wrong track.

Once you've identified answers to the questions above, I suggest sitting down with friends or family. Ask them for feedback as to what they believe your strengths and weaknesses are, relevant to both your work skill set and interpersonal interaction. They may point out other nuances of your profile which you may not have considered or been aware of.

Next, identify any companies you may really want to work for and why?

In this digital age, graduate professionals are often spoilt for choice as to the vast number of companies they could potentially work for. Yet, without any work experience, it is still a gruelling process to land a job with any of these companies. A starting point when identifying relevant, prospective employers is to look at the company mission, values and actions. Do these echo with your own beliefs? If yes, this could be a potential!

For example, Nedbank is all about saving the planet and being the "green" bank. Coca Cola is about "enjoying every moment", Spar is about being the family-values driven grocery store and Investec is about being different from the norm and unique. Which of these ethos's most resonate with you?

Do your homework! From my own experience and according to international research, doing your homework on prospective companies right from the start will contribute to a more successful job on-boarding experience, once the offer is signed. This can guarantee a far more positive, long-term work experience. Why? The more knowledge you have, the more informed you are, the more satisfied you are likely to be with decision you make. When making a quick or sudden career decision, most job seekers sit with regret, or worry about the choice they made.

When considering an offer from a company, right at the end of the job search process, one of the more significant concerns I encounter with candidates is the "What if?" question. What if this company ends up retrenching me in 12 months? What if the team hates me? What if my boss turns out to be a monster? What if they won't give me flexi-time?

Never base life decisions on "what if" or on other people's experiences. Do your own homework, up front, on prospective companies. Don't base your decisions on one bad experience, which a friend, colleague or long-lost cousin endured, in one tiny division of a much larger company. Take your time and be detailed in your approach. Doing your home on your future employer is of the first, and one of the most crucial, steps to the next stage in your career.

Start by **making a list of possible companies or industries** which do the type of work which you want to be doing and which share your values. This is a good starting point. For example:

1. BP, Sasol, Engen
2. Vodacom, MTN, Cell-C
3. FNB, Nedbank, Capitec
4. Software development companies (Microsoft)
5. Consulting companies
6. Hospitality environments
7. Etc.

Next, is to identify who might be your strategic partner, your Subject Matter Expert (SME), to these various companies?

Here comes the most difficult part. Now you need to do some research around who you can align yourself with, to the benefit of your job search. In a corporate environment, this could include individuals with similar outlooks, ethics, morals and backgrounds. Or, individuals who are higher up in the ranks and are connected to other individuals who you believe are the gatekeepers to your next opportunity.

On the corporate side, I recommend meeting with lots of people and having lots of "coffee chats"! Learn as much as you can about key stakeholders in the role or prospective employer, and establish who your allies and opponents are. This is the corporate game or corporate politics of which you must be very aware of, going into any business! Try your best to understand the corporate hierarchy and be careful about pushing boundaries too quickly. If you come across as too ambitious, or, too much of a threat, you might get stopped in your tracks very quickly.

Meanwhile, don't become anyone's lackey and don't get stuck. The second your hiring manager prevents or blocks you from flourishing or developing any further than a certain level or skill set, you're stuck. There is a difference between being stuck and being comfortable. Stuck is when you can't move, and it is generally beyond your control.

On the other hand, being comfortable is when you get used to a certain rhythm or safety net, and you're paid just enough to keep you satisfied, so you don't bother looking at other options. At least for the moment. You never want to get too comfortable (much harder to move) and you definitely never want to get stuck.

Either way, the longer you stay in the same position with the same company, the more niche your skill set becomes and the more difficult it becomes for you to adapt to new environments. Whether true or not, when a hiring manager looks at a CV, comparing someone who has remained in the same role for four, five or six years, versus an individual who has changed roles every two to three years, the latter is often perceived as the "better" and more dynamic CV. But, this is profession dependent and I speak from my experience in technology-specific vocations (business analysis, software development, quantitative analytics, data science, etc.)! I assume if, for example, you were a doctor, accountant, auditor or other, the less you move jobs, the better.

Alternatively, should you decide to pursue your job search with the assistance of an agency recruiter rather than going it alone, you also want to identify key stakeholders in your relevant field. You want to work with someone who shares some common interests and experience. This should be someone who understands your pain and what you do; i.e. your industry or specific job skill set. This individual would have key industry contacts relevant to you and be able to champion you to prospective employers, on your behalf.

Work ethic and feedback are also incredibly important and required. If your agency recruiter never provides feedback, avoids your calls and doesn't bother to tell you where he or she might be sending your CV (if they have sent your CV at all...), this is a concern. Unfortunately, no matter where you go there will always be unscrupulous characters, individuals who cut corners and/or downright "no-go" recruiters you need to avoid.

In the same breath, there are also those agency recruiters who will go out of their way to assist you in your job search. Once they understand your profile and the value you could offer their specific clients (your prospective employer/s), this could be become an invaluable relationship. If they are indeed a rock star recruiter themselves and help you shoot the lights out in terms of opportunities and steps in your career, then you will probably want to work with them multiple times throughout your career journey.

Finding your strategic partner/s may take some time, but I recommend keeping at it. Some strategic partners may only show value in months or years to come. Keep accumulating as many contacts as you. Once you have individuals who you know *will* champion your cause on your behalf, the recruitment process gets a lot easier.

"Communication must be HOT. That's Honest, Open and Two-way."

Dan Oswald

SURVIVAL TIP #5: Engaging with the Recruiter!

Below are a few steps to guide your search in finding the best agency recruiter to champion your job search. Should you decide not to use an agency recruiter and to go straight to companies, you will still be required to meet with an in-house, company recruiter. The information below can be applied to an interview with either an agency recruiter, or an in-house recruiter at a prospective employer.

Step #1: Evaluate and identify which recruiters are advertising the most opportunities for your specific criteria and/or industry.

In the case of agency recruiters, this may include one or two specific recruiters for specific industries or roles. To determine the correct in-house recruiter to talk to, you might need to take a more generalised and company-specific approach, according to which companies you want to work for, which are advertising roles specific to your skill set.

Either way, in South Africa, I suggest going onto LinkedIn or Indeed.co.za. What these two websites do is that via their job search function both sites pull several jobs from their own job board, as well as multiple other job boards across the web. Depending on the key words used in your search, the more specific or broad the results will be. For example, job search key words could include: "site foreman", "chartered accountant", "receptionist", or "java developer".

Step #2: Get in touch! Pick up the phone and remain persistent.

Recruiters are very busy people who are always overloaded with work and often running around like headless chickens. You will most likely **not** get hold of them on the first call. Yes, you can leave a message and some people do respond to messages, but often they don't. It's up to YOU to remain persistent.

Once you get hold of the recruiter, introduce yourself, tell them why you are calling and tell them that you specifically want to work with the specialist recruiter in your field. It important during this initial telephonic interaction to make a good impression and to answer any initial questions from the recruiter in detail.

If the recruiter is satisfied or needs more information, they will likely ask you send through your CV. You need to make sure you get the CV to them as soon as possible. If you only send your CV to the agency recruiter in a day or weeks' time, they may have already forgotten about you.

In addition to your CV, I recommend including specific details around projects or initiatives you've been involved in (see Survival Tip #2: <u>CV TEMPLATE</u> for more details), plus any academic degree certificates or academic results which you might have. The recruiter will ask you for this information at some point, so you might as well send it up front. It saves time and it shows that you are prepared (especially the information around projects or initiatives), which already reflects positively on you to the recruiter.

Step #3: Prepare diligently for your interview with the agency recruiter.

Remember: this person is going to represent you to the job market. If you don't take your initial interview with them seriously, they won't take you seriously. The more prepared you are, the more likely they will want to help you. Find out what documents you can send or complete in advance to make the process easier.

Step #4: During the agency recruiter interview, be forthcoming and disclose the truth.

Most agency recruiters take their jobs very seriously. If you've done your homework and chosen the right person to represent you, then providing the most accurate information will certainly boost your application, versus those of your fellow job seekers. If there are any issues from your past which might creep up, inform your recruiter up front.

It's horrible when a nasty surprise happens at a much later stage in the interview process. At such a point, your agency recruiter must backtrack with the companies they've represented you to. Again, this can damage relationships and may have long-lasting negative repercussions for both yourself and the agency recruiter, with the various companies.

Some things you should always disclose include: credit record defaults where there are judgements (i.e. it has gone to court), criminal hits on your criminal record, being dismissed from any past employers, and so forth. If you don't disclose this information up front, you appear dishonest. Don't be embarrassed! Many people have their issues and quirks. By providing your recruiter with all the relevant information, they can decide how to tackle each potential problem with a plan.

Step #5: Salary and wage discussions – be prepared.

The recruiter will ask you about current and anticipated earnings. It's one of the trickiest questions: what do you believe you are worth and will the company pay that amount? If you reply that you want a market-related salary, you might end up shooting yourself in the foot. A "market-related salary" is a commonly referred to and often fictitious term which companies use so as not to divulge salary and/or to not create any specific or unrealistic expectations on behalf of the prospective employee.

I say "often fictitious" because there are occasions where the proposed salary range was indeed based on benchmarked market data, but this is not always the case. Rather, the proposed salary is (often) based on comparing the salaries of members in the specific team or division in which the vacancy falls, which already biases the potential salary range. Then, most managers refuse to make offers to prospective employees of more than 10% to 15% on top of that individual's current cost to company (CTC), even if the individual is already underpaid.

What is market-related in one company might be ridiculously expensive or inexpensive in another. It is all about perception.

If you are a first-time job seeker, most companies have an entry salary or internship remuneration range for the lucky few who make the cut. Some salaries or stipends are great and some are not so great. Some roles, which are often pure experiential learning, may pay absolutely nothing.

Ultimately, if you are currently struggling to find a job, or worried that you may struggle to find a job once studies are complete, you need to decide on an amount you can survive on now, and then secure work experience. If you cannot get a salaried job, what else could you be doing to get work experience? Volunteer! Work for free at your local restaurant (tips only), lecture students, provide after-school tutoring, do sales on a commission-only structure for companies, etc.

Coming back to your salary discussion with your agency recruiter: there are many factors to be considered when determining a person's salary. For example, the industry worked in, location and travelling distance, results received during their qualifications and any pre-existing experience already gained. Leverage off the knowledge of your strategic partner. Ask the recruiter to explain what they believe to be your next possible salary.

If you disagree, explain why and (I recommend) provide an excel breakdown of living expenses, upcoming increases or bonuses and current earnings, to support your assertions. Encourage your recruiter/s to push for the highest possible, but agree on a realistic number and don't suddenly change your mind without informing your recruiter. The more information the recruiter is equipped with on your behalf, the more enabled they are to champion your best interests.

Telling a recruiter that "I want a higher salary because I deserve a higher salary, that's why" or "because my friends are earning this much…" is irrelevant. You or your recruiter will need to justify your anticipated amount to your future employer. The hiring manager might just laugh if you tell him or her that you deserve to earn as much as your friends, unless you can present any real substance to the argument.

Step #6: Ensure you understand all the details and clarify expectations right from the start.

It is up to you to ensure you know where your recruiter wants to send your profile and where *you* want them to send your profile. If you don't inform your recruiter of specific companies, specific roles or specific industries that you would like to work in, you can't expect them to read your mind. Clarifying expectations up front will save both yourself and the recruiter a lot of unnecessary time and disappointment, whilst drastically shortening the job search process.

Again, I cannot stress this enough: Ensure you know exactly where your CV is being sent. This will avoid potential pitfalls around CV duplication and/or being sent to companies for the wrong job.

Once a relationship with your recruiter is established, allow them a few days to get going. If your recruiter comes back to you quickly (within a couple of days) with possible interviews or additional exciting opportunities, you have a winner. If they don't and they seem to be avoiding your phone calls, WhatsApp messages and/or texts, don't waste your time. Look for someone else to work with.

The process of finding and engaging the relevant recruiter, whether in-house at prospective employers, or within an agency, is tough. You probably won't come right the first time. However, once you've gone through the motions a couple of times, it quickly becomes apparent whether a recruiter offers a quality service or not, and whether they are actually relevant to your requirements. Like when you try out an Apple iPhone versus a Samsung Galaxy, you need to determine which works best for you!

"If you want to go fast, go alone. If you want to go far, go with others."

African Proverb

SURVIVAL TIP #6: All about who you know – use those Networks!

By now you should have your CV in place, possibly have your strategic partner or partners, and you should be all set to get going on social media. Next step: networking!

But hang on… What if you've found a great recruiter who is *already* getting things going? You don't need to do any networking of your own, do you? Yes and no! You never know where your next amazing opportunity will come from. Don't discount the value you also bring to your job search (current and future opportunities). Always, also build your own networks.

Whether you are the extrovert or the introvert, the more you network, the greater the range of opportunities which may become available to you. Going back to one of my comments from the introduction to this book, whether you want to be the gung-ho, ambitious corporate-ladder-climber, or you want to obtain great breadth of work experience, following the Survival Tips in this book will enable you to do either. Your own interactions could bring a lot of value to the job hunt. Even if just preparing you for potentially uncomfortable conversations, these interactions help to get you out of your comfort zone and more able to "sell yourself".

If networking doesn't come naturally to you, it can be quite scary. You might not push yourself to meet new people or experience unfamiliar settings because that means change or feeling awkward. Networking often means putting yourself into an uncomfortable, unfamiliar situation and many people don't want to go through that.

Unfortunately, if you don't learn how to network as soon as you can, it could be disastrous for your career. When you close yourself off to new networks, you are isolating yourself and your frame of reference. Your frame of reference includes all the sources of information, including people, from which you draw conclusions and make decisions about your own life. This includes decisions regarding your work expertise, work-life experiences and ways to improve upon your current skill set.

By keeping your network small and isolated, you could be excluding valuable and influential individuals who might just have a massive impact on your current or future career decisions. If you want to grow your career and identify other opportunities you might not even have known about, then it is time to learn how to network.

Networking: time to market yourself!

Thinking back to Survival Tip #2, I want to emphasise the point I made about learning how to sell yourself and becoming your own brand ambassador. If you don't champion and campaign your own personal brand through your networks, what is the likelihood of someone else (other than your agency recruiter and a couple of close connections) doing it for you? Zero. It is time to learn how sell yourself to your networks and to potential, future employers.

The easiest way to start selling yourself is by leveraging off current networks and promoting your actions and behaviours. You need to connect to industry professionals in your space. You want to make yourself that person others would gladly refer to their friends, hiring managers or to possible job opportunities. How? Without going into too much detail, let me provide some context.

The knowledge and the values that we, as human beings, take from our different experiences in life are our *social constructs*. These experiences, both shared with other individuals and completed on our own, are what makes us who we are. This also enables one to interact with others; whether its spending time with family, having a coffee with a work colleague, reading a book, involved in charitable activities, watching a series, or some good old fashioned "me-time".

Each experience adds to our *frame of reference*, developing and entrenching our social persona which we then present to the world; i.e. whether you are more timid or reserved in some situations, versus being more loud, fun and flamboyant in other situations, with other people. When it comes to your personal brand, networking and marketing yourself to others, your social constructs and frame of reference have a big role to play!

It takes years to build up *your personal brand,* your behaviours in different situations and the commonalities, or frames of reference, which you may share with other like-minded individuals. These aspects of your character and ways in which you respond to different situations, are your personal brand. Many people don't even realise what their own personal brand is, until they start with a little bit of introspection; looking within themselves to better understand themselves.

Your personal brand is the image and the persona that you want others to acknowledge and respect. Your personal brand is what enables you to hold conversations with others, identify prospective network contacts and "market yourself" to these network contacts. Networking is not just something which people develop overnight. It is a skill which must be practised and learnt. It's hard work and requires persistence. If you take anything from this book, it should be: (1) to build and continuously review your personal brand, and (2) to train yourself to perform on-going (at least weekly) networking activities.

Why? Because if you can get that right, then you are already more than half way there. If you can build a personal brand with which you connect to network contacts, you will become a magnet for those individuals in your industry, let's call them talent scouts, looking for potential. Finding and securing a job is very much about who you know. There are many qualified candidates in the job market and not enough jobs. If you (or your recruiter) has the right connections, you've got your job search sorted!

BUT! Once you've established a personal brand and networks, you must continuously grow, nurture and protect your brand and your networks. Your reputation in the work world is everything. It is very difficult to come back from tarnishing that.

One of my favourite quotes, per Warren Buffet:

"It takes 20 years to build a reputation and five minutes to ruin it. If you think about that, you'll do things differently."

The same principle is true for you: to continue developing and protecting your networks, your behaviour and activities must remain consistent. Once you've created a brand and have a social following, you are under the spotlight. One step out of line, morally, ethically or otherwise, and you may face serious consequences.

Marketing yourself: social media networking

Effective networking requires on-going networking activities. These activities enable you to reach larger networks (i.e. more people), beyond your existing social circle. Using social platforms, such as LinkedIn, Facebook, Twitter, Instagram, and more, are the perfect ways to get going on your networking.

Social media networking is all about increasing your followers and/or your direct connections. Some platforms are a lot easier to navigate and far more user-friendly than others. The type of network you want to reach (professional or personal) will be determined by which platform you use.

For example, traditionally, many individuals used Facebook for connecting friends and family, as it is perceived as an interpersonal platform where *personal interactions* take place. Yet, the concentration of target audiences has become a lot more diverse, enabling Facebook to connect individuals to businesses and vice versa.

Facebook has become an engine able to maximise the value of the billions of users it currently connects, worldwide. This makes Facebook a far more prolific player in the social media realm, within the business marketing and advertising space, for both large and small companies, alongside all the personal interactions; the perfect mesh of business and personal. Facebook also shares the title (with LinkedIn) of one of the largest sourcing pools in the world for recruiters, of prospective candidates!

Moving along, both Twitter and LinkedIn are far more focused on business interactions, professionals and companies. There is some personal interaction on Twitter and it is a decent application to use, but other applications are becoming more popular in the personal, social, digital media space; i.e. Instagram, Snapchat and more. And, although I absolutely love using LinkedIn, it is one of most difficult platforms to derive immediate, unpaid value from, whereas Twitter and Facebook open the channels of communication to all.

Side Note: I am a big fan of LinkedIn and it's taken me years to learn all the in's and out's. I provide LinkedIn training to companies wanting to grow their LinkedIn prowess, whether for growing connections, building a brand, sales, or marketing and business development. With LinkedIn, one must be very, very specific and targeted. If not, you may struggle to find any relevant connections at all! There are several nuances or tricks which make using LinkedIn essential to any avid networker or job seeker.

Needless to say, there are various platforms and applications available, for various uses; whether sharing stories, experiences, identifying target markets, tracking down long lost relatives and more. Regarding business or professional networks, LinkedIn is my No.1 recommended social media platform. Although I've already covered LinkedIn connections in **SURVIVAL TIP #3: If you're not online, you don't exist,** I will provide a quick recap, plus I will provide a brief description around how to engage with potential contacts on LinkedIn.

To start a conversation with a potential, prospective employer or network contact on LinkedIn, you must be directly connected directly as 1st Connections. It can be very difficult to get individuals to accept your connection invite on LinkedIn if they don't yet know you. If you send too many connection invites to prospective network contacts, which are declined, then LinkedIn will send a warning message. This will include something around fair usage policies and not connecting to people you don't know.

Alternatively, you can make use of the paid "Premium" packages which allow you to send a certain allowance of direct "InMails" to individuals you are not directly connected with. These packages are super expensive! If you are a 2nd or 3rd Level Connection to individuals on LinkedIn and do not have Premium access, thus unable to send InMails, then the only way you can send a direct message to someone is if you are members of the same LinkedIn Group.

LinkedIn Groups are a whole different story, but basically how it works is: Let's say you find someone you want to connect to on LinkedIn and/or chat to, but you can't directly connect to that person. All you do is to check what LinkedIn Groups that individual is a member of, by scrolling right to the bottom of the individual's LinkedIn Profile page. Almost everyone is a member of some group or another, as this is part of the initial joining application that every single LinkedIn user goes through when they initial sign-up for their LinkedIn accounts. Once you've identified the groups, then you go to the LinkedIn Group's Profile Page and click "Join"!

Once you've been accepted into the Group, which will happen because most Groups want to grow their membership numbers on LinkedIn, you navigate to the LinkedIn Group Profile Page for that particular Group. On that profile page, there will be a Search Bar (middle, left hand side of the computer screen) which allows you to search for individual Members of the Group. Then! You should see a little envelope next to each Member's name when you hover over their names. Ta da! You can then send your prospective network contact a direct message. ***Please note:*** *LinkedIn does limit the number of direct messages you can send via groups on a monthly basis.*

The other option, is to start your networking expedition by "Following" people you want to connect with. Often, these individuals will then "Follow" you back or even request to connect.

Once you've started building up a bit of a network, start sharing content. One, two or three posts a week is OK. However, if you want to be a more avid networker, try posting at least once a day and make sure you also comment on, Like or Share other LinkedIn users' posts. Make individuals within your network feel appreciated and thank those that provide feedback. This will your network's attention and enable you to start building real connections with individuals. Once these real connections are established, you've built a sound network that will then continue delivering value for you, whether via referees, opportunities and more. Then: maintain, maintain, maintain!

When posting, I recommend being very wary of putting up any questionable posts. These include racist remarks, inflammatory statements, anything to do with politics, religion or gender. These are no-go topics! The last thing you want is for a future employer to come across a post where you went off the rails or made inappropriate comments. This could severely limit your job hunt and, once again, tarnish the reputation you have so painstakingly developed.

For example, towards the end of 2016 I stopped following one of my industry connections, a recruiter in the USA. Why? He became incredibly negative and open in his agreement with Donald Trump's approach to his US election campaign. This connection posted a picture which contained disgusting racial slurs and called for the banishment or imprisonment of all illegal aliens living in the USA.

I was furious and I wrote this individual a mail, telling him to keep his opinions to himself. I also stopped following him on LinkedIn. But before I did that, I noticed an influx of responses by other individuals in his network commending him for the picture and perspective. He gained followers who agreed with that particular viewpoint, even if that wasn't necessarily his intention. You definitely want to avoid the risk of that happening!

Bringing this chapter to a close, networking is about developing relationships through existing social circles and launching yourself into completely new experiences. Yes, you can rely on your agency recruiter, but the skill or ability of building your own networks, is invaluable. Networking ability will enable you for the rest of your life.

You don't need to know a lot of people to get started and you just need to continually practise a few consistent, networking activities, which may include reaching out, connecting to relevant people, commenting on certain types of posts in line with your work experience or industry, and sharing content which speaks to your expertise. Demonstrating that you are an engaged social media user will keep you front of mind with your networks.

"If you do not take control over your time and your life, other people will gobble it up. If you don't prioritise yourself, you constantly start falling lower and lower on your list."

Michelle Obama

SURVIVAL TIP #7: It's time... DOMINATING the Interview!

Congratulations! You have come very far since Survival Tip #1. You might think that after all the hard work that's already gone into this process, getting your attitude in check, sorting out your CV, identifying your strategic recruitment partner, building your own personal brand and networking, that the next stage should be a piece of cake? Wrong.

Realistically, the interview is the most difficult and most stressful stage in the process. It is now time to get out from behind your computer, take yourself out of your comfort zone, and to learn how to sell yourself in a real-life situation. If you're interviewing for a particular job, which you are desperate to secure, and you fail at this stage, then all the previous work you've put into the process will be for nought. Then you must start all over again!

First a quick recap:

<u>Survival Tip #1: Attitude is everything and now it is time to live it.</u> The second you walk into the building of your potential future employer, you are on interview. How you behave, how you treat other people and whether you are a match to the company culture. No matter whom you interact with, remember to show integrity, treat people with respect and to act with genuine friendliness. Whether speaking to the receptionist, acknowledging a potential executive in a suit or greeting the tea lady, remain humble, keep eye contact and put that toothy smile on display!

When hiring managers are looking for a new resource to add to the team, they want someone who is going to add value and who will fit into their environment. If the way you behave in the prospective employer's environment is not consistent with the persona you are trying to sell, you will be caught out. Remember, these people interview hundreds and thousands of individuals every year. They can tell when someone is lying and they can smell arrogance from a mile away.

Get your act together and remember that you still have a lot to learn; that's part of the reason you're there to get a job, isn't it? One day you will be able to add real value. Right now, it's time to impress, keep an open mind and show that you are a sponge ready to learn and give back.

Survival Tip #2: Putting together a ROCK STAR CV to shoot the lights out. The rock star CV you created and which is sent to the company, is the company's first impression of you. You need to live up to the profile positioned. The interview panel are going to confirm facts presented in your CV and they will ask you for examples.

If you are working with an agency recruiter, it is vital that you get a copy of your CV which was presented to the company. Agency recruiters often do a quick copy and paste of your original CV content and put into a format of their own. It is up to you to ensure all the facts are correct. Additionally, make sure you are aware of any other considerations the agency recruiter may have included in your CV; current or anticipated salary, notice period, results of any background checks, references, academic results, reasons for leaving past employers, etc.

81

If you come across any errors in the agency CV which was presented to the prospective employer, you need to make your recruiter aware immediately. This should be done before the interview so that the agency recruiter has enough time to inform the client and send through an updated version of your CV. There is nothing more embarrassing and upsetting than going into an interview and constantly repeating yourself, "No that's not correct – I never did that" or "No… where does it say that?"

When in the interview, you need to be prepared to talk about the projects listed in your CV. The projects which you listed in your CV, are what tell your story to the prospective employer. If your agency recruiter is on top of their game, they will should inform you as to what makes the hiring manager tick; what gets them excited about a prospective candidate! At the same time, don't waffle. Candidates often become incredibly passionate when speaking about their projects and go off track, not properly answering an interview question.

When talking about your projects, identify that which is relevant to the hiring manager and/or company and focus on communicating that experience. Make sure you also mention or highlight any transferrable skills, which you are aware of are requirements for the role. And, always bring it back to real examples and real experiences you've had.

For example, you might work on a particular part of the supply chain in your current company, which is relevant to the hiring manager's environment. Or, you might have worked on, or developed, a mobile rewards application, which is something your prospective employer has in the pipeline. Or, you audited the financials for several automotive companies, which means you have some understanding of how automotive businesses operate. Although the prospective employer might not be in the automotive industry, but is in another similar industry (manufacturing of some sort), you may then highlight transferrable skills you've attained, which could be applied to their environment.

I've interviewed many candidates who didn't bother to prepare for the recruitment agency interview with me. Depending on how these candidates behaved when I addressed their lack of preparation, I either refused to represent them to my clients, or gave them pointers as to how they could up their game. At the end of the day, if you, the candidate, don't bother to prepare for the meeting with the agency recruiter, how can the recruiter be confident in your abilities to "wow" the client? You are an extension of their reputation to their clients; a reputation they must protect at all costs! If you are serious about job hunting, you need to treat each interaction just as seriously.

SURVIVAL TIP #4: Starting your Job Hunt - getting ahead of the pack through strategic partnership and **SURVIVAL TIP #5: Engaging with the Recruiter!** These chapters covered a wide range of questions you need to ask yourself when looking for a new job, including some self-evaluation, and how to engage with a prospective recruiter (aka gatekeeper) to gain access to the opportunities you want.

When performing self-evaluation, of these questions included identifying what you want to achieve, what job markets you want to work in, what potential companies your skill set is a possible match to, and making things happen. If you want to get ahead of the pack, particularly at the interview stage, you better do your homework on the prospective employer and the role.

There are three key questions you need to ask yourself before attending any interview, including your agency recruiter interview! *These questions are also valuable when starting your networking expedition.* These include:

Question 1: Have you done your homework on the company?

This includes the company history, key milestones, current exciting projects or achievements. Would you be able to use this information to provide your interviewers or network contacts with motivation as to why you want to work for their company and why you believe yourself to be the best person for the job?

Question 2: Have you done your homework on the individuals?

This includes researching your interviewers or network contacts, using social media, the web and any other sources of information you can get your hands on, to ensure a fair understanding of their individual backgrounds and what makes them tick.

Side Note: *If you are requested to attend an interview and don't have a comprehensive interview breakdown of who you are meeting with, where and for what role (an Interview Confirmation, usually sent via email or SMS), you need to request this immediately from your recruiter. If you don't get the information before the interview and you are not adequately prepared for the meeting, the employer is not going to blame the recruiter... they will blame you! The recruiter is* *not the one applying for a job, you are.* **You** *need to ensure you equip yourself with the tools to ensure your interview is a success.*

Question 3: Have you read and understood the company's vacancy, and can you provide accurate examples in line with the job specification?

This includes examples relevant to both your skill set and the job description, doing preparation around projects you've completed, any initiatives you were involved in, no matter how small, and practise, practise, practise!

A stumbling block to company vacancy descriptions include generic job specifications ("job specs"), of which there are many floating around in almost every single corporate I know. Generic job specs are role descriptions used countless times across a business to describe roles with the same, or a similar title, which allow for standardisation of certain role profiles; i.e. a software developer, an accountant, a business analyst, a financial manager, a deal structurer, a revenue optimisation specialist, a human resources manager, and many, many more. Although the responsibilities and nuances of these roles may fundamentally differ on various levels, or from one business unit to another, the same generic job spec is used.

For example, just think about company external job adverts you've seen it posted online. How many times have you seen a company post a job advert which looks exactly the same as another job posting for the same company, but in a different business unit? It even looks as though the exact same wording was copied!

The reality: generic job specs exist in almost every company. It is up to you to get all the information you need to make your interview a success. This includes obtaining the correct job specification even before your CV is submitted for a role!

Unfortunately, agency recruiters don't always get it right and aren't able to secure you the information you so badly need to make your interview a success. To make matters worse, junior agency recruiters are often inexperienced, recent university or college graduates who couldn't find any other job! These individuals are provided with a phone, a computer and access to various job boards (Careers24, PNET, etc.). They barely understand the roles they are working on and rely on keyword searches to track down prospective candidates for roles.

Thus, the buck stops with you. It is up to you to ensure you are a fit for the role and adequately prepared for the interview. Otherwise, you might attend the interview and find out that the role is not the right fit, that you are inadequately prepared for your interview, or that you are not interested in the role and would not have attended the interview if you had all the information up front! It can be quite embarrassing and a complete waste of time for yourself and the interview panel. The responsibility lies with **you** to ensure you have all the correct information upfront.

SURVIVAL TIP #6: All about who you know - use those networks!

Whether preparing for an interview or building network contacts for future interactions, building your own networks is essential! Yes, you might have the most awesome agency recruiter, ever! But, that doesn't mean they will be there for you forever. You also need to become self-sufficient and competent in growing your own networks, which will be there for the rest of your life.

By building your own networks, you are enabling yourself to connect to other like-minded individuals, share information and create sources of knowledge for yourself, and develop network contacts which may turn into future prospective employers or colleagues. For example, if preparing for an interview now, where you can leverage off network contacts you've already established to obtain the inside scoop, this information could be what sets you apart from the competition!

Furthermore, when a hiring manager finds out that a candidate was asking a lot of questions and doing their homework on the role, company or division, they get excited! This demonstrates that the prospective employee has passion and goes the extra mile right from the start. An informed, curious, tenacious, humble and intelligent individual is a hiring manager's dream candidate.

Whether working with an agency recruiter or directly with the company, if you want to set yourself apart, whether as an expert in your field, an avid networker or to remain current, it's up to you to develop networking habits! These habits will have both immediate and long-term benefits. In addition, building an informative and accurate networking profile will open you up to the potential of prospective opportunities being presented to you by companies or agencies, who come across your social media profile. Thus, you are in control of establishing and determining potential, future points of contact for employment opportunities!

Moving on… time to DOMINATE the interview!

Every single step in this book is in anticipation of equipping you with the tools necessary to make a success of that critical one-hour interview. From developing your CV, developing your personal brand and doing your homework on companies, to identifying specific jobs of interest and network contacts. Yet, after all that effort and before you even get to the interview, you can still blow it!

I hate discussing this point, because I honestly cannot believe that job seekers still allow this to happen, especially when unemployment is so high and jobs are so scarce, but unfortunately it does... **Punctuality: Running late or no-shows at interviews**. If someone ran late for a business meeting with you, without informing you in advance, or they just didn't bother to arrive, without explanation, how would you feel? What would you think of that individual?

Communication is crucial! An interview is your first *in-person* impression of yourself to a company. If you are running late, you must either let the agency recruiter or the company know, at least thirty minutes in advance. If you are unable to attend an interview at a company, you must inform your recruiter **hours** before the interview... not just fifteen or thirty minutes before! That is just poor planning and will reflect badly.

There is so much work which goes into setting up an interview with a candidate. Whether coordinating interview panel members' diaries, sending an interview confirmation to the candidate, interview preparation with the candidate, arranging building access or parking, and more. It's a lot of work! By providing the recruiter with enough time, they can then contact the company, apologise on your behalf and reschedule the interview to a later date. This also enables the panel members to reschedule their diary for that day.

When an interview is setup with you, it means that the valuable and expensive time of the interview panel is booked out... for you! Companies calculate their annual, financial budgets based on the hourly cost of their staff. When there are three, four or five panel members required to attend a single one-hour interview, that is three, four or five hours of expensive company time. If the job seeker doesn't arrive, that is company time (which equals money) down the drain!

Below, I've included some of the potential consequences of not arriving, or arriving late, to your interview. Hopefully this illustrates how crucial your attendance and communication during the interview process is:

1. The company representatives are frustrated, annoyed and upset with both the candidate and the agency recruiter. It shows poor planning, a lack of respect and general inadequacy on the part of the recruiter, the job seeker or both.
2. The agency recruiter's reputation with the client is damaged because they are perceived as unable to "manage" their candidate.
3. The recruiter might be really worried about the candidate, in case something did in fact happen to you, but must first do damage control with the client.
4. The company may allow the agency recruiter or yourself to reschedule the interview, if the excuse is viable. However, it the late notice has already left a bad taste in everyone's mouths.
5. The rescheduled interview is cancelled, because the company meets another candidate in the interim. Or, the

hiring manager is so jaded by your previous no-show, that instead of wasting their time with someone who didn't bother to keep everyone informed the first-time, they then change their mind about meeting with you.

To avoid such consequences, ensure you always have the mobile number of your agency recruiter or company contact for when you are on your way to the interview. If you are running late, let your contact know immediately! This could be your dream job. The last thing you want is to upset your prospective employer before you've even met with them. People never forget a first, bad impression of a person.

Interview questions you MUST prepare for

Regarding the interview itself, I've included a list of essential questions below that you need to prepare for, leading up to any interviews.

What is your notice period? / How soon can you start?

A very general and straightforward question. You really ought to know what your notice period is; thirty days, four weeks, a calendar month, two weeks, etc. If you are not working, I would advise giving yourself at least a week to get your life in order, before starting a new job.

If you are unsure of your notice period, find out. When you provide your prospective employer with the wrong notice period information and they then want to offer you the job, only to then find out they'd have to wait an additional month before you can start in your new job, it can be incredibly frustrating. It shouldn't kill the deal, but it'll probably really annoy your future employer and can be quite disappointing. It demonstrates poor planning on your part and could push back project deadlines they might have. Ensure you have the information upfront. You don't want to start your new job on a negative footing.

Do you have any dependents?

This can be a straightforward question, or a trick question. The employer might want to gauge whether they need to make any provisions such as flexi-time or time away from the office, should your child fall ill. Yes, the world is changing and flexible work schedules are becoming the norm. At the same time, some hiring managers are still living in the stone ages and could be biased when considering work life versus home life, even when they may have their own families. The hiring manager may want to see right from the start whether you are committed to giving them 110% of your time and effort.

I advise answering truthfully and then stop talking. Depending on how you read the situation, you could ask the prospective employer if they have any children of their own. Don't try to explain why you have kids or that you will go above and beyond your family commitments for your work. This is life. Everyone has a family, whether extended or immediate. If this hiring manager only wants staff who are focused on the job 24/7, then this probably isn't the right place for you.

What are your thoughts on having a family?

This question is totally inappropriate. In most cases, if an employer did ask this question, it could land them in very hot water. For example, if an organisation is found to be prejudiced against individuals with families, or those who want families, the company could very easily be taken to the relevant labour courts by either current or prospective staff. The employer might want to see your level of commitment to the job, or they might genuinely be interested in whether you want to have kids. But, this is an interview and not a social; it's really none of their business.

If you do answer the question, keep it short and don't become confrontational.

If the employer doesn't ask this question or any questions relating to your future family, do NOT bring it up. For example, I once worked with an individual who told her employer that she planned to get pregnant later that same year. She did not get the job. Whether she was legitimately not the best candidate for the job, or whether the employer was concerned about having someone new start on the team who would be taking maternity leave in a few months' time, we will never know.

You don't want to deceive your future employer, but life happens. Personal matters such as family planning are your personal matters, not the prospective employer. It's up to you to decide whether now is the right time to consider a move in your career or not. Regardless, several companies include maternity leave clauses in their employment contracts which protect the company from a new employee starting in a job, only to then go off on paid maternity leave a few months later.

What are you currently earning?

Another straightforward question. Answer honestly and inform the prospective employer of your total cost to company (TCTC). Your TCTC or CTC is the total amount of money that you currently cost your company, which includes your (1) monthly salary, (2) any perks and fringe benefits (medical aid, pension or provident, cell phone, travel, dread disease and disability cover, etc.), (3) any mandatory contributions that the company makes on your behalf (unemployment insurance fund [UIF], pay-as-you-earn [PAYE] tax and skills development levy [SDL]), (4) any potential shares or share options, (5) a guaranteed 13th cheque or performance bonus, and more.

If you do have shares or share options, ensure you understand difference between the two. Ensure you obtain your latest statement detailing the amounts which would be due to you, and when they would be due. For example, the dividends which are payable to you via share options held with your existing company may only become available in three, four or five years. Should you leave the company before those periods, you would forfeit your share options.

Most share options or company share schemes are a method for retaining star employees for a period of years. For example, if you've got money waiting to be paid out to you, over a certain period of time, you likely won't leave your current company until all the money is paid out to you, unless a prospective employer is prepared to "buy you out".

If you have a bonus or increase due soon, ensure you inform your recruiter, whether agency or corporate. I recommend providing a comprehensive breakdown (excel works well!) of your current earnings and expenses, plus minimum expectations. It is up to you to guarantee your financial obligations are covered, whilst achieving an increase. When it comes to the money, accurate and detailed communication is vital! Clarify those expectations up front!

What is your anticipated salary?

Be very careful with this question. The biggest deal breaker when hunting for a new job is money. If you are working through an agency recruiter and already discussed salary with your recruiter, make sure you have crystal clear clarification of your and their expectations regarding anticipated salary (refer to: *Step #5: Salary and wage discussions – be prepared, in Survival Tip #4)*. If the interview panel do ask you about anticipated salary, then refer the interview panel to your agency recruiter to discuss anticipated salary, to avoid any salary miscommunication.

Sometimes agency recruiters may increase or decrease your proposed anticipated salary for different clients. Don't assume that they do this to cheat you. Rather, if the agency recruiter is doing their job properly, they are factoring in additional expenses you may have (travel, loss of certain benefits, etc.) and/or leniency on the prospective employer's side regarding budget or job grading. Make sure you know what financial figures are communicated, to which clients. This way, you are prepared for the potential eventuality of discussing salary in your interview.

So how do you come up with an anticipated salary?

Even though a candidate may understand their current TCTC, they are often horrendous at working out their anticipated salary. Several reasons for this, including: they don't understand all the factors involved; they are biased in their own favour; they believe in negotiating from a high starting salary; they compare their salary to their colleagues' or previous friends from varsity; or they may believe that the top end of the salary ranges, as advertised by companies on job postings, are what they will earn if they land the job.

Many job seekers believe that the top end of the anticipated salary range advertised on the job posting is what is referred to as a "market related" salary. Thinking back to your initial interview with your agency recruiter and as discussed in Survival Tip 4#, a market related anticipated salary is very much a matter of perception. This perception can easily change depending on the scenario, the environment or industry the candidate comes from, the years of experience the individual has, the qualifications, the references, and more.

Quick Recap from Survival Tip 4#:

A "market-related salary" is a commonly referred to and often fictitious term which companies use so as not to divulge salary and/or to not create any specific or unrealistic expectations on behalf of the prospective employee. I say often fictitious because there are occasions where the proposed salary range was indeed based on benchmarked market data. From what I have seen, this is not always the case. Rather, the proposed salary is based on comparing the salaries of members in the specific team in which the vacancy falls, which already biases the potential salary range. What is market related in one company might be ridiculously expensive or inexpensive in another. It is all about perception.

When it comes to salary, to avoid doubt or misunderstanding, you must already have discussed your expectations in a firm and open conversation with your recruiter. Most likely, your recruiter informed you that the average increase in salary which you can expect to achieve is between 10% to 15%, in addition to your current total cost to company (TCTC). When discussing anticipated salary with a recruiter, consider any advice they may provide, present reasons as to why you believe you deserve your specified salary range and come to an agreement on a proposed salary you would *definitely* accept, all other factors being equal or compensated for. Then... allow them to do their jobs on your behalf!

It is incredibly frustrating to work with a job seeker who states one amount to the recruiter, yet communicates an entirely different message to the prospective employer. In such a scenario, the candidate ends up looking like the bad guy, or it casts doubt on the agency recruiter's abilities. For example, for the job seeker, it appears that you can't make up your mind, that you go back on your word, or that the recruiter representing you does not know what they are doing. It reflects negatively to the prospective employer and should be avoided.

If you can't come to an agreement on anticipated salary right from the start and insist upon negotiating at the end of the recruitment process, you leave yourself open to disappointment. Why? Because, companies always look at their bottom line. If you state that you want a market related salary or *"let's see what they put on the table"*, you are allowing companies free reign to offer you as low as possible, which enables the company to keep their costs down. It isn't fair, but that's business.

Whereas, if you clarify expectations upfront and come to an agreement with the relevant recruiter or company, then those expectations can be communicated from the get-go. This will save everyone a lot of time and disappointment, especially in a situation where the company would not have offered you what you wanted anyway. I cannot stress it enough: clarify expectations upfront!

During an interview, the interview panel is generally perceived to hold all the power versus that of the job seeker. For example, they have the power to make or break your chances of securing the job. It can make the interview an incredibly stressful experience. Whenever I work with new job seekers, I always brief them to **not** discuss salary in the interview.

When you are the one setting the bar, you can't take back what you have said. It doesn't matter whether the amount is too high, too low or, just right, you have committed to a number. If an individual is not properly prepared for their interview regarding the money question, they tend to shoot themselves in the foot. The job either undersells or oversells themselves. Should you then wish to change your mind at a later stage, it may reflect negatively on you.

Some sage advice I once received, never commit to a decision when you are under pressure! When under pressure, we tend to make rash decisions influenced by our immediate circumstances and with only limited information. This is the opposite to taking your time to analyse the information available in a more relaxed setting and choosing the appropriate answer, which is in your best interest.

Unfortunately, ol' Murphy often throws a curveball. The prospective employer may adamantly ask what you would like to earn, even if that monetary figure was communicated prior to the interview. There are numerous reasons why the panel might ask about money during an interview. They might want to negotiate with you and see how you cope. They may wish to re-affirm salary expectations right then and there, so that they can hold you to those expectations in the future. Or, they may want to ensure that the agency recruiter has not upped your salary to a much higher amount, of which you are unaware. Whatever the reasoning, ensure you and your recruiter are on the same page!

Reasons for leaving past employers

Reasons for leaving questions must always be treated very carefully. If you are working with an agency recruiter, double check the CV which the agency recruiter sent through to the company on your behalf. The CV should contain specific reasons for leaving each previous employer or role, and your current employer.

Ensure you are happy with the reasons for leaving, but beware of making the reasons too specific. When future employers have a new vacancy to fill, they tend to review hundreds of CVs before they make a shortlist. If any of the reasons for leaving on your CV seem strange, absurd or too relevant to their own environment, they may not even consider taking your application further.

What makes it trickier, is that the hiring manager often does not make the first call on CVs. The company's in-house HR or corporate recruiter does the shortlisting. If the in-house recruiter sees anything out of place on a CV and the job seeker is not an out-of-this-world candidate, they might just delete the CV. Not only are the reasons for leaving important, but so is the accuracy of your CV, the relevance of your profile to the job applied for, and the grammar. For a recap on CVs, see **Survival Tip #2: Putting together a ROCK STAR CV to shoot the lights out!**

An example of a reason for leaving which may affect your job search negatively includes: There is a prospective employer who would like to hire a sales person. The prospective employee will earn a commission-only package and will be expected to do a lot of travelling to visit clients. The job seeker will most probably not get an interview if the following reasons for leaving are listed on their CV:

a) "Moved closer to home. The travelling was just too much." Or,
b) "Job was unstable. Worked on commission and could not afford to pay the bills."

If the prospective employer is looking for someone who will travel and earn commission-only, then either of the above reasons for leaving could result in immediate disqualification from the process. Furthermore, the prospective employer might gain the impression that the job seeker is not the best sales person and not the right fit for their job, because that job seeker was unable to make enough money to survive on a commission-only package.

Another reason for leaving to be particularly careful of is **money**. When it comes to money, employers seem to lose all common sense. Although wanting to earn more money is a completely valid reason, whenever a candidate mentions the pursuit of a greater salary, they are considered greedy. This is crazy, I know! Most hiring managers themselves *wish* they could earn more money. However, there appears to be a natural bias against prospective employees who appear to *"only be in it for the money"*, even if that's not the case.

Further reasons for leaving to avoid include:

c) "Not happy with my current salary and looking for an increase."
d) "Don't believe I am paid what I am worth."
e) "I believe I am not earning a market related salary. My friend is an employee at Company X and we studied together. She earns way more than I do..."

Never compare your salary with that of friends or colleagues. You will always be disappointed. There are many variables which influence what your friends or colleagues earn, versus what you earn.

For example, their results achieved at University for certain subjects, versus your results; the topic of a project they completed at University which is relevant to their current employer; any specific previous employment experience they gained during or after university; any specific system or project experience gained; the employer they work for might offer higher salaries than that of other companies in the market; the individual's skill set might be highly sought after by the specific division they work for; or, maybe they just caught a lucky break!

In conclusion, when it comes to dominating the interview, the following pointers are particularly important:

1. *"Failure to plan, is planning to fail"* (direct quote by Benjamin Franklin). You must do your homework before the interview. This includes researching the company, the job, the interview panel members, any key initiatives the company may currently be involved in, the industry the company is in and more.
2. It's good to make some small talk at the beginning of an interview, but avoid any family or personal questions where possible. Certain questions and answers around

your personal circumstances are inappropriate and irrelevant and should be avoided.

3. Be prepared to discuss your previous experience, including detailed breakdowns of key projects or initiatives for which you were responsible and which are relevant to the role you are interviewing for. Furthermore, be prepared around your reasons for leaving.

4. Even though prospective employers really shouldn't be discussing salary in an interview as it can seriously disadvantage you, be prepared. Know the numbers of your current and anticipated salary. If working with an agency recruiter, rather tell the prospective employer to discuss your salary expectations with the recruiter, as you do not want to disadvantage yourself in the interview, by either overselling or underselling yourself.

5. If the prospective employer does not bring up money, then you must not bring up money. Stay away from that topic in the interview! You want the employer to evaluate you based on your skills and not just on how much you cost.

6. Finally, and I haven't mentioned this previously, but be prepared for potential logic questions. Not all employers or interview panels do this, but there is an ever-increasing trend emerging where prospective employers ask candidates very random, logic focused questions and/or case study scenario questions, to better understand an individual's thinking process. The employer is not necessarily looking for the right answer, but rather how you attempt solving the question. Don't let it knock you off your game.

For example, a question I've been asked myself: If I had to use the little, wooden ice-cream sticks which come with individual ice creams (Mega, Magnum, etc.), how would I go about measuring the distance from Pretoria to Cape Town, as the crow flies? Tough question. It is not about getting the answer right. It is about displaying a step by step and logical approach to how you solve the question.

"When you focus on problems, you will have more problems and when you focus on possibilities, you will have more opportunities."

Kamari aka Lyrikal

SURVIVAL TIP #8: The last mile – critical success factors as you near the finish line

The end is close and your job search ordeal is almost over! Hopefully by now your job search is ending, or you're feeling more prepared for what's to come. You might have finished the necessary interviews and about to do a psychometric assessment. Or, you've completed the whole process and you're awaiting a decision by the company. There could still be one or two hurdles to come and these should be taken just as seriously, as all previous stages in the process.

Psychometric testing

A psychometric assessment is generally the last stage in a prospective company's process, before deciding which candidate to offer. Most psychometric assessments include language, logic and numeracy components. Psychometrics come in different forms. Many include a combination of multiple choice questions, case studies, pictures, diagrams, and more. In addition, most psychometrics are timed assessments and require individuals to complete them within the allotted time.

In a psychometric assessment, there are no correct answers. There are only indicators of specific behaviour patterns, as scientifically tested for in past research. Psychometrics inform the company whether you, the prospective employee, would fit into the company's environment and culture. It goes beyond the skills, knowledge and qualifications which one may possess and looks at personality and behaviour patterns when faced with certain stimuli or scenarios. Additionally, a psychometric assessment reviews your ability to learn or adapt to your environment.

Every company looks for a different fit. Some companies want individuals who are more extroverted, outspoken, gregarious and driven. Others, might prefer a more deliberate, logical and analytical approach. Culture-fit can vary from department to department. Culture-fit also informs the hiring manager as to your personality and behavioural responses when confronted by other personality types in a team. Some personality types just don't gel well together and the hiring manager needs to decide whether they are prepared to take that risk, or not.

If requested to do psychometrics after completing all the interviews, this is a good sign. For many companies, it signifies the last step in the process. Before completing the psychometric, you must prepare. Ensure you have a good night's rest and a big breakfast. If possible, try organise to complete the psychometric first thing in the morning. The more alert and awake you are, the better. Find out which psychometric you are completing and the duration. There is a lot of information online regarding different types of psychometrics. Remember to breathe, do whatever preparation you can, and take along some water and food, especially if it is a full day assessment.

Psychometrics are not particularly difficult, but they do force the individual to think. If incorrectly answered, the person administering the test (the psychometrist) might pick up what is known as a "false positive". A false positive happens if it is detected that the individual completing the test, answered a question or questions out of character from a pre-existing pattern of questions, already answered by that individual.

For example, if the job seeker tried to guess what the most likely "correct" answers might be. Job seekers often do this because they want the job so badly and try to guess what attributes the company want in a prospective employee. But beware! A false positive is not a good thing. It essentially means that you lied and/or tried to cheat. If caught with a false positive result, you would be disqualified from most recruitment processes.

Keep the interview process going

Once one interview or recruitment process for one job has come to an end, don't just suddenly stop job hunting. During the interview process with one company, go for multiple interviews with other companies or divisions within companies. Unless, and even if you are the hottest thing since sliced bread, you cannot assume you've secured the first job you interviewed for. Furthermore, when there are so many interesting companies and so many exciting opportunities available, don't limit yourself to just one job, especially if you have other interviews incoming! Why not do yourself a favour and see what else is out there?

I always say to my candidates: there is nothing the wrong with keeping your options open. The more options you have, the more informed the decision you make, when you do finally decide which job to take. Don't make decisions when other people are putting you under pressure and definitely go for interviews at a whole range of companies. Allow yourself the time to see at least some of the options out there.

At the same time, if you do really love an opportunity, take it! If that job is the one, don't waste time! Another candidate might just swoop in and you've lost the job.

Attending multiple interviews can be difficult and time consuming. Few job seekers inform their bosses that they are looking for a new job. Many don't want to cause suspicion in their work environment and thus try to minimise time out of office. This can make the recruiter's job quite difficult, specifically when trying to setup interviews at the strangest hours to suit your schedule.

Unfortunately, if you are the one that wants a job, you are the one that needs to compromise and not the other way around (unless you were headhunted for a role). Be clear with the relevant corporate or agency recruiter regarding possible, suitable times. When those times cannot be achieved, compromise. The more *you* are the one rescheduling interviews, the worse it looks to the company and your recruiter.

The wait...

Interviews, excitement, meeting new people and new companies! Psychometrics, even more excitement! And then... silence. The last stage in the job search process is always the most frustrating. The larger the company you interviewed with, the longer the wait. Sure, sometimes things happen quickly! Most of the time, you are left waiting and wondering, second guessing yourself and your performance during the interview. Those feelings can quickly turn into annoyance and impatience. Why hasn't my recruiter said something? What if I wasn't good enough? Has the recruiter disappeared off the face of the planet?

No, no and no. I am just as guilty as many other agency and corporate recruiters when it comes to keeping track of the many interview processes for different candidates, and constantly providing feedback where required. Although I personally believe in a more candidate-focused approach to recruitment, versus a vacancy-focused approach, most recruitment companies in South Africa survive on achieving high volumes; the more candidates placed, the more money they make. Thus, the more candidates for one role, for which an agency recruiter achieves interviews, the higher the likelihood of placing the role. When working with such volumes, there always tend to be candidates left behind and without feedback.

Then again, sometimes your recruiter might just be really, really busy! I remain in contact with most of my candidates and several of my clients via WhatsApp. Sifting through Outlook emails can be a nightmare and instant messaging is a lot easier! If you pop your recruiter a quick SMS or WhatsApp to request feedback, I bet they will respond! Whether it is because the recruiter knows you can see when they are online, or because instant messaging is that much faster than email, it always works for me.

In addition to no feedback or a very busy recruiter, **the wait** is the period during which the company is finalising procedures on its side. There might be other candidates being interviewed, or the company might be awaiting results from various psychometrics. Or, if the company is keen on you, they might be trying to get paperwork finalised to put together an offer, which itself can take days, or even weeks to complete.

Alternatively, the role might suddenly be put on hold and the recruiter hasn't had a chance to let you know. Unfortunately, this happens often! You think you've got the job and then POOF; it's gone.

My advice: remain in contact with your recruiter, stay calm, be patient, attend other interviews and try not to annoy your recruiter, the company or both. If you completed a proper vetting process with your recruiter and know they are doing everything in your best interest, including keeping you informed up until this point, let them do their job. If you don't hear from them for several days, pop them an instant message!

The wait: bypassing the recruiter

There are times where I can legitimately say that candidates have done some very frustrating things, which have the potential to undermine the recruiter. For example, I've seen numerous situations where job seekers bypassed the agency recruiter and went directly to the company to find out where the hold-up is the process is. For some candidates, this may seem like the logical thing to do, especially if your recruiter doesn't have any new information for you. On the other hand, it makes your recruiter LOOK BAD to the company and even indicates that you don't trust the recruiter to do their job properly, on your behalf.

Often, corporate or in-house recruiters become very annoyed with the agency recruiter, should job seekers contact them directly. The agency recruiter is expected to manage the candidate relationship, whilst the in-house, corporate recruiters manage the relationship with the hiring manager. Certain processes require certain steps to be followed. Just imagine if you were working for a company and bypassed your direct line manager to start interacting with the next level up in the hierarchy. This might really upset your line manager and it's just not on.

Please don't get me wrong. I am a big believer in transparency and minimising hierarchy. However, the role of the agency recruiter is to act as the representative and intermediary to the company, on the job seeker's behalf. If the agency recruiter is truly working on your behalf, then they are doing everything in their power to get you the best opportunity and offer possible. When bypassing the recruiter to go directly to a company, you leave yourself at risk of ending your relationship with the company very fast, and/or missing out on the service and assistance your recruiter can provide you with, and/or alienating either your recruiter or the company.

Often, agency recruiters also shield the company and the candidate from one another when it comes to the more blatant conversations, where either the hiring manager or the candidate might just tell the other party to go take a hike. Recruiters play the middleman role (the mini-psychologist to both sides), handling, negotiating and mitigating risks on behalf of both parties. Often, there are issues which need to be clarified, additional "coffee chats" which need to be had, and small, niggly things which stand in the way of a successful placement of the individual with the company.

For example, whenever a candidate completes an interview, I always phone that individual for interview feedback, so that I may provide this to the company. This enables me to continue the engagement between the corporate and the candidate, beyond the interview. On behalf of the job seeker, I then push the process along, encouraging feedback from the company. Once I receive feedback from the company about the candidate, I relay this to candidate. Depending on the feedback given, I then relay that feedback in a constructive manner to the candidate. If the company is keen on the candidate, I continue pushing that process forward.

Regarding the interview feedback: human beings are very sensitive creatures and we all have different perspectives and interpretations of events. What a candidate might say about an interview on one day, might be a completely different perspective the next day. The same is true for hiring managers. Sometimes the candidate might be an immediate no. Other times, the hiring manager may realise how lucky they are to acquire a certain resource, but only after interviewing a whole pool of candidates.

In summary, what often happens when a candidate and company interact directly, is that processes get shot down very quickly, especially if there is a communication gap or misunderstanding between either party, because there is no buffer. Unfortunately, hiring managers and corporate recruiters just don't have the time or capacity to look after (i.e. babysit) each candidate who comes for a job interview. Thus, agency recruiters play a vital role in managing the candidate relationship, whilst developing, nurturing and managing the expectations on both sides.

Furthermore, where the agency recruiter might be able to provide valuable insight and experience of dealing with a particular in-house, corporate recruiter or hiring manager, the candidate does not have this knowledge or experience. Thus, the field is wide open as to what happens next. Furthermore, if the company suddenly starts re-requesting information, such as salary expectations and the like, the candidate could end up in a difficult spot.

For example, the candidate might be totally unaware of what was previously discussed between the agency recruiter and the company. The candidate then provides "new" expectations which could either lead to the immediate end of the interview process, or, the company takes advantage of the situation. The candidate might state a lower salary expectation, which does not cover all their costs, and then find themselves in a tricky situation.

Remember: the company is sitting in the power position, not you. Without an experienced recruiter by your side, you may quite easily lose or give away some of your bargaining power, out of desperation to secure the job. If working with a recruiter, trust them to do their job on your behalf!

Background checks, references and all other documents

Depending on the company processes and the agency recruiter you are represented by, you will undergo background checks as part of the initial stages in the recruitment process. If not, then these checks are absolutely vital before any corporate, and most definitely any blue-chip companies, will make you an offer. These background checks include a full screening and verification of the validity of:

a) Your South African ID or national passport (or other nationality if applicable);
b) Any permits if applicable;
c) Various formal education certificates, specifically matric, degrees or diplomas;

d) Your credit record or credit status, including any judgements against you; and
e) Your police criminal record, or lack thereof.

These background checks, or a variation thereof, are standard practice throughout the South African job market (and international job markets). Thus, before starting your job hunt you need ensure you have copies of your ID, degree and matric certificates on hand, as these will be required to confirm the various background checks.

In addition, if you do have a criminal record, ensure you have a copy of the police docket or certificate, stating exactly what it is that you have an infringement on your record for. The details around criminal records can take up to eight weeks to come back from the relevant authorities. By that time, you could have lost the job to another candidate.

Another standard practice in the recruitment industry is the presentation of contactable references on behalf of the candidate to the prospective employer. This generally happens either right at the beginning of the process, or as part of the massive pack of documents required by the company, when they are considering putting together an offer for you.

As part of your references, please do not put down personal references (brothers, sisters, aunties, uncles, etc.) and certainly not your pastor. Employers want references of past employment, including hiring managers, work colleagues (preferably more senior than yourself), clients or superiors whom interacted with you and can attest to your abilities.

If you are a recent school leaver or university graduate, it can prove quite difficult to provide references, unless you already gained part-time work experience whilst studying. If you have no past work experience, I suggest asking your University professor or a past teacher to write a reference letter for you, which specifically speaks to your abilities, drive, aptitude for learning, and the role you played within teams and especially on teamwork assignments. Then, rather than your professor or teacher being bothered by hundreds of phone calls or emails, there is one letter which recruiters or companies can refer to.

Finally, the last set of documents which are required by prospective future employers include details around your medical aid, pension or provident fund, any forms of insurance which your current employer pays for on your behalf and/or any type of shares or share options which you might have with your current employer. Ensuring you have this information ready for the agency recruiter or company when the time comes, will enable smooth and that expectations are managed.

The offer...!!!

FINALLY!!!

After much ado, waiting and stress, the offer arrives! This can be an amazing, okay or disappointing experience.

I always say: you cannot take back a candidate's disappointment after a company has presented a disappointing offer to a prospective employee. Thereafter, even if the company does up the offer, the individual is just going to think to themselves: why couldn't they offer me the higher number in the first place? Thus, getting the numbers correct up front and managing expectations throughout the entire process, is fundamental.

Never think that a company might surprise you with a little bit extra. It almost never happens. Occasionally, hiring managers put together better offers than expected, yet ultimately the cost of your salary eats into their corporate budget. The lower the salary a hiring manager can hire a new resource at, the better for their budget. If you received a higher salary than you were expecting, it is because your recruiter motivated like crazy on your behalf, and/or you or your in-house recruiter did a good job of negotiating on your behalf.

When companies put together offers for prospective employees, I always request a mock or dummy pay slip which I may send onto the job seeker. The mock pay slip is a representation of the average, approximate monthly salary which the employee can expect to earn, factoring all perks and benefits which that person would receive in their new role. If the relevant recruiter has done their job properly, then the mock payslip should adequately reflect the included perks and benefits which the employee currently receives, plus the additional take-home or net salary which the prospective employee will receive after all deductions. This net or take-home salary is the cash which is paid into the employee's bank account on *payday.*

When looking at a job seeker's current payslip versus that of a mock payslip, the question I always ask myself is: will this person be able to continue affording their current lifestyle and still receive a decent increase? If not, and unless the job search is purely focused on finding a better role rather than more money, then considering offers which are below what the prospective employee is currently earning, would just not make sense.

Some of the most important items to note when reviewing the offer letter or employment contract are as follows:

a) Prospective start date and whether this is negotiable?
b) What is the new Total cost to company (TCTC)?
c) Eligibility for and date of next annual review and bonus?
d) Eligibility for any other incentives?
e) Number of annual leave days plus other leave provisions (family leave, sick leave, etc.)?
f) Working hours and flexi-time?
g) Any restrictions on employment such as restraints of trade and/or restrictions on interacting with certain companies in a work capacity?
h) Any additional perks or benefits not necessarily included in the TCTC but which make up the experience of working for that particular company? For example, free DSTV if you work for Multichoice, a free cell phone if you work for MTN, or preferential interest rates (prime minus 2.5%) on certain lending products, if you work for one of the banks.
i) Company policy around further studies and study allowances? Often this is not included in the offer letter or employment contract and such information needs to be requested.

If you have any questions, or you are unhappy with your offer, you must speak up. However, if the recruiter obtained the salary you asked for, or more, and you do really like the opportunity, be very careful about changing your mind at the last second. Every action you take sends a message to your recruiter and to the prospective employer about you. When considering an offer which is everything you asked for and more, be careful about suddenly becoming greedy.

Unless you are an absolute super star, the hiring manager most likely has a potential second prospective employee in mind. If negotiations with you go south, then the hiring manager can simply change course and begin the offer process with another candidate. If you truly believe the opportunity is the one for you, then be wary of negotiating for the sake of negotiating, especially at the last second. You could lose the job.

The dreaded counter offer!

Then comes the counter offer. Whether you intended to obtain a counter offer or not, they happen all the time. Why? Companies are desperate to retain quality staff and it's a lot cheaper and easier to retain an existing resource (at least until another resource is trained up...) who knows the current projects, systems or processes, versus going through the entire recruitment lifecycle again.

The three main types of counter offer approaches include (1) hiking up an employee's existing salary in their current environment, with or without a lock-in, guaranteed bonus, (2) playing the loyalty card and/or (3) promising and even guaranteeing that the departing employee will get that job they always wanted!

Sadly, some people have no problem playing companies up against one another, no matter the damage to existing relationships. They are just in it for the money. If that's you, then a financially motivated counter offer can be a fantastic thing!

However, if you really are keen to begin a new chapter in your work life, then the "emotional, loyalty card", or the "we will give you that job you always wanted", appeal might be the more dangerous and silent killer. It is only when it gets to crunch time, once individuals must resign, that you realise how tough it is to leave your existing employer. If you've build solid relationships with your team, it's even worse! Your existing employer or team may beg you not to leave. They might say things like: "We're building something together!" or "You can't leave now. This place... or I won't survive without you!"

Be careful. You will start questioning your decision to resign and take your new job. Even if your current employer does or doesn't put together a better financial offer, many individuals are swayed by the emotional appeal to accept a counter offer and remain within their comfort zone. Then, only a few months later, to find themselves left alone by those same colleagues who begged them to stay, who themselves (the colleages) were offered better opportunities elsewhere and didn't accept a counter offer. What now?

You've burnt bridges with the company where you received the initial offer. The company or hiring manager probably won't consider you again, because your actions demonstrate that you are an unreliable and unethical individual. This can have far reaching consequences in any organisation, considering that people talk. Recruiters and hiring managers are likely to warn their colleagues about that prospective employee who defected at the last minute. In addition, your agency recruiter might be quite frustrated with you. After all their hard work, going through the entire, tedious recruitment process, for you to change your mind at the very last second, no matter what the reason, it is frustrating and exhausting. Again, it reflects poorly on them to the company.

When it comes to counter offers, just don't do it! If you take a counter offer, there are repercussions. You will regret it and you will probably be back on the job market in under six months. You need to ask yourself: why did my company not value me before? Why is it that when I am walking out the door, they suddenly have the money to throw at me? Why am I doing this? Who am I doing this for, the company or me?

To which I respond: It's cheaper to retain you, than to replace you. See counter offers for what they are; a cheap, last-minute retention strategy which hardly ever work. Once an employee has made up their mind to leave, they are no longer invested in the success of the company. Do you really want to work for a company if you've already made up your mind to leave? Do you really want to work for a company that uses last minute tactics to keep you where you are, versus encouraging you to spread your wings?

How does the agency recruiter get paid?

You've got your offer in hand and you are super excited! Heck, you want to sign immediately. But wait... do you now have to pay the recruiter or how does that work?

Overseas, in the United Kingdom and the United States, the agency recruiter generally receives payment from both the candidate and the company, especially for senior positions. In South Africa, this is not the case. In South Africa, candidates are spoilt. Recruiters will fight tooth and nail to represent quality candidates to companies, because the recruiters know they have a guaranteed placement in hand.

In South Africa, the company pays the recruitment agency a percentage of the total cost to company (TCTC), aka the "placement fee", of the successfully placed candidate. The agency recruiter then receives a commission percentage of the placement fee. Different companies set different placement fee percentages and commission structures for recruiters. The placement fee is paid by the company and not by the candidate.

Resignation, on-boarding and follow-up

It's done! You've accepted the offer and it's time to resign. The clock is ticking. You need to resign quickly so that you can work your notice period and start in your new environment on the proposed start date. As you stare at the clock, you fret in agony at the prospect of submitting your resignation. You don't want to disappoint anyone. You don't want the company to think you are ungrateful. You've made up your mind and now you still need to endure another week, two weeks, 30 days or calendar month in your current environment.

Resigning is never easy and this is when most counter offers take place. Either, your employer tells you to wait and then brings someone else more senior into the room to convince you, or your boss asks you to please meet the next day for an impromptu meeting to discuss your decision and the options available. If the counter offer doesn't work, your hiring manager will try buy as much time as possible, to get you to finish off certain initiatives for which you were responsible, before letting you go or allocating you somewhere else.

Again, the loyalty card plays a role. Whether because of history, morals or your work ethic, you don't want to leave the company in the lurch and are more willing to delay your departure so that you leave on good terms. There is nothing wrong with that and it is the respectable thing to do. But, beware of being taken advantage of during this time. It isn't your fault if your current employer doesn't have good business continuity in place. In my opinion, you've made the decision to leave. Do your job to the best of your ability, don't kill yourself trying to finish off each little task, and move on with your life sooner rather than later.

During your notice period your prospective employer may reach out to you to begin the on-boarding process. This is the process of loading your personal details onto the prospective company's payroll system, allocating your new employee number and uploading any vital documents required, in line with the company policies. In addition, during the on-boarding process you should find out more about the company fringe benefits and perks, which would be relevant to your monthly salary; medical aid, pension and/or provident fund, etc. A benefits consultant at your new company will normally discuss these fringe benefits with you, whilst you are completing any further required documentation.

Once all is done and dusted, you finish working your notice period with your current employer and prepare for the next chapter in your life. Before starting in your new job, your agency recruiter or the company should be in touch to welcome you and to provide you with the **first day details**. This includes by what time you should arrive on your first day, whom you should ask for on arrival, anything you might need to bring with you to the office, and anything else for which you should be prepared. Technical equipment such as your access card, laptop, a corporate cell phone or 3G dongle, as required by your role, tends to be arranged by the company technical support team.

Then it is time to start.

As an agency recruiter, I always pride myself on maintaining relationships with my candidates throughout their careers. Thus, I often state that the way you can determine the quality of a recruiter is by evaluating the extent to which they follow-up and remain invested in the employee's wellbeing and success in their new job. Unless the recruiter has changed jobs or recruitment specialisations themselves, those recruiters who are fly by night and disappear once the deal is done, are not individuals you should work with again.

Rather, every step in the recruitment lifecycle is an opportunity for you to evaluate your recruiter and to decide: is this my recruiter for the rest of my career? Will he or she help me take the next steps needed to reach the next level? If yes, then remain in contact and keep yourself open to evaluating options which your recruiter might present to you from time to time. If not and you want to go it alone – no problem!

Bringing this chapter to an end, hopefully this book has helped guide you through your current career change and will enable you to approach each next career step informed, prepared and ready to tackle your future!

"Life is like riding a bicycle. To keep your balance you must keep moving."

Albert Einstein

EXTRA VALUE-ADD! THE INSIDE SCOOP: What do hiring managers look for in the "best candidate for the job"?

Ever wondered how you could get the edge in your job search? Is there anything specific you could be doing to *"up the ante"* and improve your chances of securing the job? What gets hiring managers excited about a candidate? What can put you ahead of the pack?

As an additional value-add to #HireMe!, over the course of November and December 2016 I conducted my own research regarding the candidate attributes in young graduates and professionals which make hiring managers and leaders of industry tick. To conduct my research, I contacted relevant heads and hiring managers from numerous industries including but not limited to Finance, Information Technology, Telecommunications, Pharmaceutical, Engineering, and more. I asked several questions aimed at uncovering what gives young graduate professionals the upper hand in the job search process and conducted my research via emails, texts, LinkedIn messages, telephone conversations and face to face meetings.

Many hiring managers did not want to be too specific on certain criteria, stating that a go-getter personality was most important of all. However, critical and specific findings did emerge. I would like to present some of the key themes from my interactions with the hiring managers in the hopes of aiding your job search and your approach to the work world.

Please note *that my research is not conclusive, but rather to be used as a guide for students and job seekers. I also included* *some additional information about the various university programmes discussed by hiring managers, my resources including News24, TopUniversities.com, EduConnect, the World Economic Forum, and various University websites.*

Theme #1: Solid foundations and an ability to think critically.

Sadly, not everyone is afforded the same privileges or opportunities in life. For many South Africans access to basic education is a major challenge, never mind tertiary education. Furthermore, personal circumstances and social consequences may have a devastating impact on an individual's foundations which enable him or her to enter, develop and succeed in the work world, in whichever capacity. Few overcome difficult personal circumstances.

However, for those individuals who can overcome challenges and/or obtain a solid secondary and tertiary education, there are a lot of opportunities. Studying at a reputable university or college and obtaining a degree, provides you with the foundation on which further knowledge can be developed. Not everyone has a formal education and there are many people who develop their skill set via extensive industry experience.

If you pursued and completed tertiary studies of some form or another, it will certainly give you the upper hand in at least securing a job interview. Furthermore, if you can complete a Honours, Masters or Post-Doctoral qualification, there is much more academic credibility regarding your ability to think critically. At a postgraduate level, students are expected to start thinking for themselves. This includes contributing original work to the academic body of knowledge, versus spouting someone else's academic theories. Not everyone can afford to study further than a diploma or undergraduate degree, but if

125

you can, I seriously recommend it. Even though it might still take some time to secure your first job, post-graduate studies will give the upper hand in the longer term.

Here I've included some information around the degrees, courses and institutions which were specifically recommended by hiring managers and leaders of industry whom I chatted to. I've tried to condense this information as much as possible.

Per my research, the **Top Four recommended local universities by hiring managers** in the South Africa included:

a) University of Cape Town (UCT), ranked by various local and international organisations as the Number 1 university in South Africa for many years
b) University of Witwatersrand, or otherwise known as "Wits"
c) Stellenbosch University
d) University of Pretoria, or otherwise known as "UP", "Tuks" or "Tukkies"

Each university has its own specialisations for which it is renowned amongst the different hiring managers. Although not specifically mentioned by the hiring managers, the University of Kwa-Zulu Natal (Engineering and Physical Sciences specifically), Rhodes University (excellent research focus) and UNISA are also notable universities which offer some solid degree programmes and courses in South Africa. UNISA is specifically ranked in the top 20 universities on the African continent and is noted for its part-time/remote course offerings.

I've included some more details below regarding the key offerings from UCT, Wits, Stellenbosch University and UP.

But, before I get into that, I must make special mention of **North West University (NWU),** formerly known as University of Potchefstroom or "Potch" and specifically the **NWU Business Analytics, Informatics and Mathematics (BMI) programme.** I have personally interacted with many past students from the NWU BMI Programme and dealt with numerous clients who view this programme in very high regard. One of my LinkedIn industry contacts, Annie Symington (HOD: Analytics at Multichoice), highly, highly recommends the BMI programme to any hiring manager looking for quality, data-focused candidates and/or students. What I like most about the BMI programme is that it combines business, IT, mathematics and one of the greatest buzz words of the 21st century, data!

Data is the future. Whether you want to work in a more technical role which requires interrogating data, identifying sources of information and performing various mathematical or statistical calculations, or a less technical role, which requires making sense of information (analytics) and applying this information to real world scenarios, data is everything. Businesses make both operational and strategic decisions based on the data or information available; what product to develop, which customer complaints to handle, what division to retrench, when to hire and when not to hire, etc.

In addition, all the financial information which goes into bookkeeping or accounting spreadsheets is financial data. The information which individuals in social media, public relations or marketing related professions use, to communicate with the public, is a form of data which needs to be understood and interpreted. Performing any kind of research requires understanding how to utilise qualitative or quantitative methods for interpreting data. Even throwing together a basic excel spreadsheet for your own personal budget, requires you have some knowledge around arranging data. Needless to say, I'm quite passionate about the topic of data!

Coming back to NWU's BMI Programme: this is quite a technical programme, but for anyone wanting to pursue a career in data, mathematics, analytics, statistics, IT or actuarial sciences, I highly, highly recommend it. **In my time as a recruiter I have placed every single one of my candidates whom held a degree from the NWU BMI programme.** Hiring managers worked with like candidates with this degree because it is rigorous, cutting edge and the individuals gain real industry experience at a Masters level. The NWU BMI degree is in definite demand.

A brochure for the NWU BMI programme can be downloaded here: http://www.nwu.ac.za/sites/www.nwu.ac.za/files/files/p-bmi/documents/Bemarkingsmateriaal/Marketing%20brochure%20for%20prospective%20students.pdf

Other **recommended data and/or analytics specific Degrees** include:

B.Sc Mathematics

B.Sc Quantitative Risk Management

B.Sc Actuarial Science

B.Sc Computational and Applied Mathematics

B.Com Statistics

B.Com Informatics

B.Com Econometrics

Recommended institutions for these degrees:

University of Pretoria (UP)

North West University (NWU)

University of Johannesburg (UJ)

University of the Witwatersrand (Wits)

University of Cape Town (UCT)

Stellenbosch University

University of Cape Town (UCT) has several excellent degree programmes across various fields. For instance, UCT is believed to have the best business school in South Africa, closely followed by University of Pretoria's Graduate Institute of Business Science (GIBS) and Stellenbosch University's Business School. UCT is also believed to offer of the best Education, Law, Biomedical, Engineering, Agriculture and Forestry, Geography and Development Studies (top 10 in the world) faculties in South Africa. It has a massive focus on research and is on a drive to become the top research institution in Africa.

Side note: Beware of studying at any institution which is too heavily concerned with achieving postgraduate scholars, versus creating work-ready young graduates. Many institutions are motivated and funded for each postgraduate scholar they produce. Thus, their motivation lies in creating more academics. When considering any university programme, do so with your eyes wide open.

Wits University has in recent years upped the ante with its staunch Business School and Finance offerings, alongside a focus on research. Wits is also believed to provide one of the best Accounting offerings in the Gauteng area, although it competes with University of Pretoria. Furthermore, Wits was recommended to me for its Physics and Actuarial Science offerings.

Stellenbosch University is believed to be top notch with regards to its Engineering degrees, Life and Earth Sciences, Mathematics and its Business School. The Stellenbosch University Business School is ranked in the top in Africa and in the top 100 worldwide for several years now.

The **University of Pretoria (UP)** is particularly famed for its prowess within the Information Technology sphere, Engineering degrees and Social Sciences, including Humanities, and Veterinary Sciences. In addition, UP, through GIBS, was the first university outside of North America to launch a Masters of Business Administration (MBA) programme. This MBA and the GIBS executive MBA are highly ranked in the Top 100 MBAs worldwide for the past several years.

Other than South African institutions, several hiring managers I spoke to emphasised that candidates should do their utmost to gain an international education, where possible. Some of the recommended certifications, such as the Financial Risk Manager (FRM), Chartered Financial Analyst (CFA), Chartered Institute of Management Accountants (CIMA), Chartered Institute of Procurement and Supply (CIPS), for example, are still reasonably costly for the average individual. Such certifications can be done via self-study. Thus, individuals do not need to travel abroad to obtain international education and costs are decreasing dramatically daily.

Another Option: Given the rise of the digital age and access to the internet, access to information is completely open, and some of it is even free! For example, international companies **Coursera** and **Lynda.com** (both completely online or via mobile apps) offer a multitude of free courses and/or free durations for courses, diplomas and certificates, all of which must be completed online. Subjects include everything from computer science, IT and software development, to finance, mathematics, business, photography, marketing, social sciences, life sciences, linguistics, personal development and more.

If you have a smartphone, the world is your oyster. There is plenty of access to relevant information and education.

Theme #2: Emphasise an eagerness to understand the connections between things and link different concepts.

If I apply this theme to the interview process, I would suggest that when you are in an interview, this is an opportunity for you to demonstrate to an interview panel that you gained experience in certain areas and can translate that knowledge and experience into solving problems relevant to the prospective employer's environment. Thus, demonstrating that you understand the connections between things, the theory and practical behind specific concepts and can apply transferable skills to problem solving.

Theme #3: Demonstrate a thirst for continuous improvement and knowledge gain.

This does not necessarily have to be via formal education, but could be by getting involved in different initiatives, completing ad hoc courses, engaging with stakeholders within other areas of the business to better understand how the work you do affects the bigger picture, working in internship or tutoring roles whilst studying, getting involved in community or social projects, and more. If you have done any of the above, you need to ensure this information is included in your CV content. During the interview this experience can be discussed as a relevant talking point when asked what you like to do during your spare time and/or to improve yourself.

Theme #4: Discuss your aptitude for learning and adaptability in continuously changing times.

Many individuals struggle with handling change. The younger generation coming through the ranks is very used to change and able to adapt more easily. Change is not only limited to structural changes within organisations, or global changes in financial markets or the environment, but to changes within companies in response to greater external and internal changes impacting the company. Ever heard someone say, "But, that's not my job" when requested to undertake a task? That is a clear example of an inability to adapt (and/or laziness).

The ability to adapt to change within an organisation is critical. Relevant to this theme, such changes include on-going shifts in job requirements or specifications, which require you to continually equip yourself with the skills required to do your job. I advise demonstrating your ability to learn and adapt to change in an interview, by highlighting how you approached different jobs, projects or initiatives. Talk about how you specifically equipped yourself with relevant skills which enabled you to do the job. Were there education requirements or interpersonal competencies? What were the challenges you faced? Was there any resistance? Did you try to learn new strategies to deal with the challenges or resistance?

Theme #5: Highlight your ability to commit and complete.

One of the major reasons why individuals with degrees are preferred over candidates without degrees, is because achieving a degree is no easy task. It requires time, effort, hard work and commitment. Depending on the degree and the time it takes, you could spend another three to five years of your life studying, before entering the work world. If you are studying towards a profession, such as becoming a doctor, accountant or lawyer, you're easily looking at upward of seven years of study and work experience required, before it becomes official. The more you can demonstrate to a prospective employer your tenacity and drive, especially when things get tough, the better.

Going back to talking about projects and initiatives during the interview, I am a big believer that any project, initiative, activity, undertaking or event for which you were specifically responsible, is what will tell your story to your future employer. Not some random, worn-out generic job description. The prospective employer wants to understand exactly what it is you previously accomplished and how that translates into what you can achieve in their environment.

Thus, to demonstrate your commitment and ability to complete, make sure you discuss the really challenging projects or initiatives, and certainly the ones that failed. This does not make you look bad! Rather, it demonstrates to your prospective employer that you know what it means to fail and pick yourself up again; to learn from your mistakes and to gain the scars, which come from years of experience. Furthermore, it demonstrates humility, that you can admit to your failures, which is a sign of a high EQ (emotional intelligence). A high EQ will always stand you in good stead with a prospective employer.

In conclusion...

There are several factors which hiring managers and business leaders consider when appointing a new employee. Even the candidate with the perfect experience or skill set may still fail in the job interview, if he or she is unable to communicate the how, why and what makes them the best person for the job. Other than any pre-existing formal education, every single one of the themes I discovered during my industry research emphasises an individual's ability to communicate; to communicate how they think critically, to discuss and apply how they adapt to changing circumstances, to describe how they demonstrate their ability to commit and complete, to discuss how they continue to self-improve, and to stress how they go about understanding and applying the link between interconnected concepts and ideas.

My last piece of advice: You don't need to be the brightest spark in to get the job. You just need to (1) properly prepare for the recruitment and interview process and (2) demonstrate, without a doubt, your ability to understand, translate and communicate your message best, in a way that applies to the job and the environment you are trying to get into. And sure, a little personality never hurt!

About the Author

Nikki Pahliney is a South African recruitment guru, "mompreneur", avid blogger and networker, member of the Businesswomen's Association of South Africa and the Black Management Forum, and a business leader in her field.

She has established and built three successful businesses from scratch, in the fields of recruitment and coaching, training and development. She has experienced wins and losses and faced the darker side of human behaviour within business, coming out on top. She holds local and international undergraduate and postgraduate qualifications and has a keen interest in research and contributing to the academic body of knowledge.

Nikki is incredibly passionate about enabling individuals and companies to unlock their potential. She is a firm believer in employee investment and engagement as a conduit to employee retention. She believes that the most sustainable and rewarding accomplishments are achieved through the milestones attained by others.

Nikki has managed to reap her success through consistent application of tried and tested methods across different industries. Although Nikki is a firm believer in sound planning and research, she will always encourage individuals to *not* get stuck in the analysis paralysis phase; rather take action, do something and learn from the experience!

She is an incredibly vibrant, tenacious, target orientated and action driven individual whose motto in life is: *"It's time to take over the world!"*

In her free time, Nikki spends time with her amazing husband, their gorgeous son and three beautiful dogs. She loves to blog and believes that through knowledge sharing she is able to assist others (and be assisted by others) in developing greater insights and solutions. She also enjoys getting involved in community focused initiatives with the aim of giving back.

Last, but not least, Nikki strives to get involved in youth development initiatives wherever possible. She is a driver for change, identifying issues in the status quo and an ardent believer in empowering individuals with the tools to make a success of their careers.

Hand in hand with her entrepreneurial nature, she is always looking for opportunities to create value for those who are struggling to get into the job market, uncertain as to where their careers are headed, or who just need a little guidance. Thus, in December 2016, Nikki initiated #HireAGrad, a South African unemployed graduates' scarce skills development initiative, focused on uplifting and connecting young, unemployed South African graduates to the necessary tools to gain scarce skills, and to significant, potential employment opportunities.

Nikki's favourite quote: "Be the change you want to see in the world" Mahatma Ghandi

www.ingramcontent.com/pod-product-compliance
Lightning Source LLC
Chambersburg PA
CBHW072139280526
45788CB00002B/701